The Collaborative Nature of Coaching

Basic Skills for Managers, Leaders, Life & Executive Coaches

By

Maura Dolan

Copyright 2021© Maura Dolan. All Rights Reserved

No part of this publication may be reproduced, distributed or transmitted in any form, or by any means, including photocopying, recording, or other electronic or mechanical, methods without the prior written permission of the author, except in the case of brief quotations embodied in reviews and certain other non-commercial uses permitted by copyright law.

Acknowledgements

There are a number of people I would like to acknowledge for their role and support in producing this book: Orna Ross who endlessly encouraged me to undertake this piece of work and who, through the Alliance of Independent Authors, patiently guided me through the self-publishing process; Niall Wallace who gave me many objective and wise observations on the flow and content; Niall Kilcullen, of Kobba.ie, for the design of the graphics and the professional service in providing several options, listening, and understanding my needs; and Richard Bradburn, editor, of editorial.ie, who painstakingly reviewed my work and offered many worthwhile suggestions.

I have drawn on many resources from other coaches in putting together this book on foundation skills in collaborative coaching. Thank you to those many coaching sources for a range of skills and tools that brings so much to the richness of the coaching process. The book is about collaborative coaching and the coaching process at a basic level; the additions of these sources enriched the understanding of the coaching process for all those starting out on this life-changing process.

Finally, to my wonderful family – Brian my husband, best friend, and eternal supporter. Colm, Eoin, and Ciara who offer so many insights and thought-provoking observations about life. Through your own achievements and eternally curious dispositions, you have inspired in me an interest to continue my own development and evolution. Thank you to all of you for being such a loving family and for all the collaborative, trusting times where vulnerability is okay and leads to open, loving, and caring relationships.

Contents

Chapter 1: What is Coaching? 1

    Introduction 1

    Definition of Coaching 2

    History of coaching 3

    Reasons and applications for coaching... 4

    Understanding Collaborative Coaching 10

    Principles of Collaborative Coaching 21

    Collaborative Coaching Competencies.. 22

    What makes a good coach? 36

Chapter 2: Coaching in the Workplace 39

    Definition of Executive Coaching...40

    The Coaching Contract.. 50

    What makes a good Executive Coach? 56

Chapter 3: The Coaching Process – How to Develop Coaching Skills and Competencies 69

    Understanding How People Learn... 69

    Collaborative coaching 87

    Questioning Skills 90

Chapter 4: More About the Coaching Process 101

    How to start a coaching session 101

    How to structure a coaching session 111

    The ARCH coaching model (Achieved, Relevant, Choices, Headway) 113

Chapter 5: Communications and Building Rapport 148

    Definitions: 148

    Communications 148

    Communications and Coaching in a Digital Age 179

Chapter 6: How the mind works, Belief Systems and Values 184

    How the mind works 184

    Belief Systems 193

    The magic of belief systems 193

    Values and fulfilment 208

Chapter 7: Concluding Coaching 219

Appendix 1 225

Appendix 2 – 21-Day Planning Exercise 229

Appendix 3 – Sample questions on how to start a coaching session . 234

Appendix 4 – List of values 239

References 246

Index 249

About This Book

The aim of this book is to serve as a guide to help coaches/managers and leaders build basic coaching skills and effective, collaborative relationships with coachees, direct reports, colleagues, and peers.

The book describes the basic core competencies necessary to achieve these collaborative relationships. It is a blend of theory and practical application of how to use coaching skills in everyday personal and professional life.

Who is this book for?

This book is aimed at people who are interested in human development, in learning about coaching and understanding the power of collaborative coaching. It will benefit those who work as external and in-house coaches, leaders, managers, and those who work as part of a team.

In the workplace, as in everyday life, there are times when it is appropriate to use a collaborative coaching process, and times when it is appropriate to mentor or to be more directive. I will discuss the difference between mentoring and coaching later in the book. However, whichever intervention is more relevant at a point in time, the more one uses a collaborative coaching style in one's communication, thus handing back the baton of ownership, responsibility, and autonomy to the receiver of the process.

My reason for writing this book

My passion for coaching started when I was volunteering on the support lines for an organisation called Parentline. One day I was working in their support centre and saw an advertisement from a Life Coach on the volunteers' noticeboard. The advertisement included a description of the role of a Life Coach. I read the description and it was a lightbulb moment for me; I knew immediately that this was what I wanted to do.

At the time I had completed a course in counselling skills and knew that, although I connected at a very deep level with the skills of a counsellor, I did not want to work as a counsellor. I set about learning all I could about coaching, immersing myself in both the development of my coaching proficiencies and the skills of training others to become coaches, and in the never-ending pursuit of developing my own self-awareness. One of the reasons I was attracted to coaching was that I was going through my own personal challenges, self-discovery, and self-awareness while navigating the challenging world of young motherhood and exploring the next steps in my career. For me, coaching was the perfect recipe; it combined my interest in people and my belief in giving people autonomy and confidence in their own skills, an ability to evaluate options, learn from setbacks, and take responsibility for their decisions. I also recognised in myself a need to do something that I was wholly connected to, where I felt I was using my strengths and adding value. For me, coaching was the perfect fit.

I first started building my coaching skills and coaching hours over seventeen years ago and that led me to achieve accreditation as a Fellow of Coaching. During my initial period of training as a coach, I felt inadequate and doubted that I was making any real contribution. Life and Executive Coaching at this point was an embryonic discipline, was relatively new as a concept, and I felt unsure both about the process and my efficacy. At one point when building up my coaching hours to become an accredited coach, I reached out to my supervisor for support. My supervisor asked me a simple question: 'How do you think your work is impacting on the coachee?' I sought feedback from Sarah (not her real name) and I still remember the response I got from her. My questions to Sarah were 'What worked well in the coaching process?', 'What would you like more of?', 'What would you like less of?'

The response I received went something like this: 'Maura, these are crazy questions. I have found the sessions so helpful. To start with, I feel listened to, that someone understands me and gets my world. I realise now that I am responsible for my own decisions and the support in finding solutions is invaluable. There is nothing that needs to be done differently.' The feedback was a key learning point for me and is the foundation of my approach in this book. I realised as a coach I needed to park my own internal judge and manage my own insecurities so that my inner critic does not inhibit my ability to coach. It also clarified for me that the role of the coach is to support the coachee in finding their own solutions – hence the collaborative process.

From my initial explorations into coaching in the 1990s to my writing of this book, I have always devoutly believed in the coaching process; it is a truly collaborative process. Coaching is forward moving, rooted in positivity, and action-based. It looks at what is working, rather than what is not working. Collaborative coaching is based on the belief that each person has within themselves the answers to their challenges. For me, these underlying principles fit with my own core philosophy: that people are capable, competent, and intelligent. The role of the coach is to support a person in exploring options and alternatives, and develop self-awareness and self-understanding to move forward and achieve their potential.

As a start, it may be useful to read the book in its entirety. However, each chapter covers a stand-alone topic that can be revisited independently of other chapters. Throughout the book I have included reflective exercises, and I encourage you, as the reader, to take time to complete these exercises and deepen your awareness of how you can apply the theoretical aspects of coaching in a practical process that will enhance your performance and deepen your knowledge.

This book is an insight to the process I use for introducing people to the fundamentals of coaching skills that can be used to enhance people's lives at both a personal and professional level, and to increase unity, cohesiveness, and collaboration in the workplace. This book is a culmination of my passion for the discipline of coaching. It is about basic skills, and my intention is to follow it with two further books: one about advanced coaching skills and one about a coaching style of leadership.

In this book I refer to the person who is being coached as the 'coachee'. This is to differentiate the individual in an executive/business coaching context from the client. The client is the organisation that hires the coach to work with the coachee. The question of who is the coachee and who is the client is discussed further in the book.

Chapter 1: What is Coaching?

Introduction

> 'Incremental change is better than ambitious failure . . . success feeds on itself' Tal Ben-Sharar, author Happier: Learn the Secrets to Daily Joy and Lasting Fulfilment

In this chapter you will:

- Learn definitions of coaching and the nature of collaborative coaching
- Learn about the history of coaching
- Explore reasons for and applications of coaching
- Compare similarities and differences between coaching and other interventions such as mentoring, counselling/therapy and consultancy
- Learn about the principles of collaborative coaching
- Complete a coaching competency schedule

Definition of Coaching

Coaching is …

… a powerful alliance designed to forward and enhance the life-long process of human learning, effectiveness, and fulfilment. – *Co-Active Coaching* (Whitworth, Kimsey-House, Kimsey-House & Sandahl, 2010)

… Client and coach become a team, focusing on the client's goals and needs and accomplishing more than the client would alone. – *Thomas Leonard, Father of American Life Coaching at Coach University*

… Evoking excellence in others. (*Flaherty 2015*)

… The art and practice of inspiring, energising, and facilitating the performance, learning and development of the player. – *Myles Downey*

… A safe place but also a transitional space where the coachee moves out of their safe place. – *Kets De Vries*

… No passengers on the bus. Coach and coachee both play their part. – *Hetty Einzig*

My definition of coaching is that it is a **collaborative,** thought-provoking process that inspires Motivation, creates Awareness and Deepens the learning. I call it a MAD process.

The coach runs this collaborative process and the coachee runs the agenda. A skilled coach will explore and understand the coachee's needs and 'meet the coachee at the point where they are' in their current situation.

History of coaching

Traditionally, the word coaching is associated with enhancing skills and performance in sports. Dave Davy, sports historian, suggests that the idea of coaching has existed for a long time. The term was first used in the 1800s to describe a tutor who supported a person through exams. The word coach describes the process of 'carrying' or transporting a person from where they are to where they want to be. The coach exists to get the best out of individuals within complex and dynamic environments. Coaching as a professional discipline began to develop in the mid to late 1990s and is an ever-evolving discipline.

According to the British Association for Counselling and Psychotherapy, coaching has become a worldwide phenomenon. It has grown organically from various fields of self-development and, in particular, the development of humanistic psychology (also known as the 'Third Force'). One view is that coaching reflects a synthesis of three movements: the growth of the talking therapies; consulting and organisational development, including industrial psychology; and the proliferation of personal development training.

Coaching is a multidisciplinary intervention in that many of its underlying principles are based on psychology, success in sports, and therapeutic interventions such as counselling and psychotherapy. It continues to develop and evolve and deepen as new discoveries such as the evolution of neuroscience give greater insight into understanding human behaviour. At the same time, the effects of coaching have begun to receive greater amounts of study because businesses and workplace health researchers want to learn more about what made coaching styles so effective. According to an article in trainingindustry.com, 2018 ('2018 Training Industry Report', 2020), the role of the facilitator is changing from one that is based in a classroom with large numbers of participants, to the role of personal coach or tutor. Learners seek personalised learning that is relatable to them.

Reasons and applications for coaching

Coaches work in a number of areas with coachees including:

- Developing self-awareness, leading to better understanding of responses to behaviours

- Understanding and controlling emotions
- Developing emotional intelligence
- Moving coachees into adult modes of working
    - Working with a coachee to identify situations where they feel powerless to change a situation even when opportunities for change are available
    - Working with a coachee to develop an adult-to-adult communications style
    - Working with a coachee to take responsibility for actions and how they respond to situations
- Examination of skills, performance, and performance enhancement
- Getting closure around unfinished business
- Developing leadership capabilities and responsibility
- Building self-belief
- Developing autonomy – the ability to make decisions based on critical thinking, and to hold on to opinions particularly in the face of opposition
- Developing a growth mindset that looks for learning in setbacks and disappointments

- Looking at life goals, questioning what gives a person a sense of purpose, connection, and meaning
- Developing a business focus, ensuring that the whole organism is looked at, not just the coachee's needs
- Developing a systems perspective where the culture in a group or team is explored and how that impacts on the individual as well as the team

While some of these themes may have a psychological dimension, they do not require therapeutic interventions; they are part of the normal day-to-day challenges of life that most people encounter. The coach works with the coachee to understand the concerns and the thoughts and feelings connected to the issue. The collaborative coach supports the coachee in coming to a desirable outcome and towards deepening learning and self-understanding.

Opportunities occur for coaching every day, not only in formal coaching sessions, but coaching over a cup of coffee, at the water cooler, and in general leadership roles on a day-to-day basis.

One of the strengths of coaching is that it can take the form of a two-minute conversation within the workplace between, for example, a manager and direct report or, alternatively, may be a formal session that can run as long as is contracted. Sessions may last sixty or ninety minutes, with some being longer or shorter. Similarly, coaching programmes may be a one-off or may run for a number of sessions as agreed during the contracting phase.

The applications for coaching are as wide and as varied as the coaches themselves.

There are thousands of niche areas and potential niche areas available within which a coaching practice can be developed. The development of the technology industry and digital age also opens up new possibilities for coaching through virtual platforms.

Amongst the more established and better-known areas of coaching are:

- Personal/Life coaching
- Career coaching
- Business coaching
- Executive coaching

Personal or Life Coaching

People come to a Personal or Life Coach to explore:

- Life planning/enhancement
- Relationships (singles, couples, families, etc.)
- Health & fitness

- Wellness Coaching
- Spiritual Life Coaching
- Creativity
- Financial freedom
- Organisation
- Challenges arising for Teenagers – Confidence, Self-esteem, Identity, Who am I?
- Challenges arising for college Students – Stress, Moving away from home, Confidence/Mindset

Career Coaching

People come to a Career Coach to explore:

- Career transition
- Career decisions
- People considering a move into a corporate role
- People struggling with the decision of whether to stay in a corporate job or choose another option
- Workplace trends
- Interview Coaching

Business Coaching

Business Coaching includes working with:

- Entrepreneurs
- Organisations, regardless of size, industry sector, or whether public or private
- Owners or managers of companies
- Start-up companies (actual or planned)
- Professionals in private practice

Executive/Corporate Coaching

Coaches can be involved with:

- HR Departments
- CEOs, executives, managers
- Companies interested in launching a coaching initiative
- Companies intending to train managers to be coaches
- Initiatives to prevent and/or cure burnout
- Coaching workshop initiatives
- Strategic planning, creating a vision

- Sales coaching
- Launching and developing teams

Current trends include coaching for working with different generations. Research suggests that the millennial generation (born between 1980 and 2000) expect a close relationship with managers, the right to have a voice and to be heard. At the other end of the generational continuum are the traditionalists (over 70, born 1945 or earlier) and the 'Baby Boomers' (born 1946 to 1964); these generations are known as the 'Third Acters'. They are looking for new meaning in work and life and often seek to reframe their working contribution rather than retire.

Understanding Collaborative Coaching

Collaborative coaching?

Collaboration is a non-hierarchical process that happens when all voices are heard and all contributions valued, within a safe and open space of dialogue.

Collaborative coaching is a co-designed alliance where coach and coachee work in a collaborative process to achieve transformative outcomes, growth, balance, and the capacity to manage uncertainty in constantly changing environments. Bedwell et al., (2012), suggest collaboration is a process and leads to outcomes, rather than being an endpoint in itself.

Coaching is a rich tapestry of interwoven disciplines, an amalgamation of insights taken from psychology, neuroscience, therapeutic interventions, philosophy, learning theories, and sports. It is a discipline whose effectiveness is grounded in theoretical concepts and models. However, its power lies in its practical application where the coach and coachee work in a collaborative relationship. The essence of collaborative coaching is about change and working in a synergistic process with individuals, teams, and organisations to identify barriers, blocks, and behaviours to making change. In collaborative coaching, the coach creates the space for the coachee to think for themselves, navigate through and explore options, be creative, find solutions, and take action.

Throughout this collaborative journey, coachees are challenged to open their minds, examine personal biases and limiting beliefs and behaviours, and to develop self-awareness. They are provoked to critically analyse performance, strategies, and systems to enhance effectiveness in both personal and professional contexts. Features of coaching such as clarifying values, supporting and encouraging new ways of acting, thinking and behaving are embedded in everyday human interactions and conversations. In addition, these collaborative conversations are a thought-provoking way of critically thinking, solving complex problems and creatively influencing culture, change, and strategy.

The catalyst at the start of a coaching journey is often when someone no longer wants things to stay the same and they see that coaching can assist in making that transformation happen. The collaborative coach hands the coachee the tools and holds the light, so the coachee can see what needs to be done and have both hands free to do it.

One of the skills in achieving collaborative coaching is to explore options with a coachee, to clarify the coachee's thoughts on what might work for them. Self-awareness and clarity come from questions such as:

- 'What needs to change for you to make a change?'
- 'Tell me what is not working for you at the moment?'
- 'What is the cleverest thing you can do at the moment to make a change?'
- 'What if you do nothing at all?'
- 'What is the first step you need to take?'
- 'Tell me about a time you managed to make this change before; what worked well?'
- 'Who do you know has achieved a similar change? What did they do?'

Comparisons to similar, though different interventions

The following interventions are frequently confused with collaborative coaching:

- Therapy/Counselling
- Consultancy
- Mentoring

Collaborative coaching is not any of the above.

Reflective Exercise

Before reading the section below, consider what you believe are the differences and similarities between the profession of coaching and the other professions mentioned above.

Collaborative coaching vs. therapy

Therapy is about looking back, remediating, supporting to explore and 'fix', whereas coaching is about performance and moving forward.

The table on the following page compares coaching to therapy and indicates the differences between coaching and therapy/counselling:

Collaborative Coaching	**Therapy/Counselling**
The Coach:	*The Therapist:*
•Supports the coachee in finding their own solutions	•May offer solutions
•Works with 'fully functioning' people and does not act as a Therapist	•May seek to remediate past problems
•Addresses: What's next? What now?	•Addresses: Why me? Why this?
•Engages in a collaborative, equal partnership	•Engages in a traditional counselling relationship
•Focuses on the future	•Focuses on the past
•Works on exploring new perspectives and possibilities	•Addresses negative past experiences
•Works with the coachee on goal setting	•Works to address weaknesses and barriers

While there are differences between therapy and coaching, the professions share many similarities:

- Both work on the basis of developing adult and responsible behaviours
- Both require strong interpersonal skills, are based on trust, confidentiality, and professional intimacy
- Both are process-driven, with the client taking ownership of the agenda
- Each is a reflective process that explores beliefs, values, attitudes, and mindsets

Collaborative coaching vs. management consultancy

Although the primary function of management consultants is to work at an organisational level, more and more are reporting that their clients are seeking one-on-one work. As a result, many management consultants are adding coaching services to their portfolio.

The following table compares coaching to consulting and indicates the differences between coaching and consulting:

Collaborative Coaching	Consulting
•The coach evokes answers from the coachee	•A consultant is expected to provide answers
•The coach's expertise is in the domain of conversation, communication and interpersonal skills and understanding behaviours – the coach does not have to be an expert in the business field	•A consultant is expected to be an expert within a specific industry or business
•Revolves around relationships	•Services are information/technical based
•The coach works regularly to support individuals during and after organisational change	•Tends to deal with specific problems. A consultant works in pursuit of organisational change and makes recommendations that are then implemented by the organisation

While there are some major differences between management consulting and coaching, the professions share many similarities.

- Both rely on communication and building strong relationships

- Both aim to support organisational change

- Both help in solving problems, setting goals, and designing an action plan

- Both can design and facilitate workshops and work with teams

In one sense, all coaches are consultants, whereas few consultants are coaches. Coaching, however, can be conducted outside of a consulting relationship.

Collaborative coaching vs. mentoring

> Mentoring: 'A process which supports learning and development and thus performance improvements, either for an individual, team, or business. Mentoring is usually understood as a special kind of relationship where objectivity, credibility, honesty, trustworthiness, and confidentiality are critical' – *Parsole & Wray*

Traditionally, mentoring was a hierarchical relationship involving a wise senior who dispensed wisdom, knowledge, and advice to a grateful but essentially powerless junior.

Modern mentoring relationships, however, are based on a more mutual, equal, and collaborative learning alliance, where mentors often use coaching techniques to help mentees develop problem-solving and critical thinking skills as well as technical expertise.

The following table compares coaching to mentoring and indicates the differences between each modality:

Collaborative Coaching	Mentoring
•Coaching creates a future, based on the coachee's desires, goals and experiences	•Mentoring creates a future, based on the expertise and experience of the mentor
•Coaching covers a broad range of goals and outcomes including: performance/professional development, changes in mindset, attitudes, behaviours and belief systems and therefore is a collaborative process	•Mentoring is usually more specifically focused on technical skills and career-advancement and is therefore a more directive process
•Coaches are regarded for their interpersonal skills, understanding of behaviours and ability to draw on the coachee's understanding of the situation and their ability to draw the answers from the coachee	•Mentors are usually regarded as experts in their field and freely give advice

Similarities between coaching and mentoring:

- Both require well-developed interpersonal skills
- Both require the ability to generate trust, support, and commitment, and to generate new actions through listening skills and powerful questions
- Both shorten the learning curve
- Both aim to improve performance and productivity
- Both encourage the individual to stretch but provide support if they falter
- Both provide support without removing responsibility

Reflective Exercise

Take five minutes to create your own definition of collaborative coaching

Principles of Collaborative Coaching

There are no problems, only CHALLENGES that you have not allowed yourself to resolve.

Every day brings the promise of a bright new beginning with the opportunity to transform every life challenge into a success.

TRYING

If you try something, you may get a result.

But if you do it, you will get a result.

TRYING is one step away from DOING.

It is the doing with a built-in allowance that you may fail.

TRYING IS NOT THE DOING OF THE THING; IT IS SIMPLY THE DOING OF THE TRYING' –

So – just do it!

Be committed to developing your coaching skills, START TODAY!

(Source unknown)

The essence of the collaborative coach is a coach who works with the coachee to develop a partnership based on non-possessive warmth and trust. The collaborative coach works on the basis that everybody knows what they need to know and when they need to know it! It's just that they don't know this.

Reflective Exercise

People come to coaching for lots of different reasons, but the bottom line is **change**. Take five minutes to reflect on the above statement.

Collaborative Coaching Competencies

The coach should be aware of and develop the following nine coaching competencies.

1. Present a Professional Image

A coach should understand coaching ethics, work within these ethical guidelines, and adhere to professional standards. Professional coaching associations such as the EMCC (European Mentoring & Coaching Council), IAPC&M (International Authority for Professional Coaching & Mentors), the ICF (International Coaching Federation), and the AC (Association for Coaching) provide comprehensive ethical guidelines and codes of conduct such as 'demonstrates respect for the client and ensures that the client remains independent of the coach' and 'engages in continuous professional development (CPD) and attends supervision in keeping with guidelines of the Professional Association of which they are a member'.

2. Setting the Coaching Agreement

This may be an informal e-mail, one-page document or a multiple-page detailed document. In business coaching, the agreement may be supplied either by the coach or the client. In personal coaching, the coach normally takes responsibility for outlining the terms and conditions. The coaching agreement should clearly outline the logistics of the coaching session: the number of sessions, duration of each session, venue, cancellation policy, and rates. The coach should also look after their own personal safety and ensure that the coaching is held in a safe location, with appropriate security in place.

In the context of an in-house coaching programme, other factors need to be considered at the contracting stage. An in-house programme needs to include clear guidelines around confidentiality, how objectives are agreed, and who has a role in setting these objectives. The organisation needs to decide, ahead of introducing the in-house coaching programme, if it wishes to identify specific business-oriented benefits that it wants to set for the duration of the programme, as opposed to the sessions being non-directive. For in-house coaching programmes, the need to ensure trust between the coach and coachee is fundamental to the success of the coaching programme, therefore the question of reporting structures and confidentiality need to be clarified at the outset.

In addition, the following points should be considered at the contracting stage:

- Who delivers the coaching programmes? In some organisations, the line manager may be appointed as the coach. In other organisations, a coachee may select a coach from a panel of qualified in-house coaches who are not aligned to their department.

- Guidelines for what the role of HR or the Learning and Development Dept. and other key stakeholders in the coaching programme are: What role do they have in aligning the organisation's perspective and goals with the coachee's perspective and goals to ensure that the coaching programme serves an organisational as well as coachee agenda?

- What feedback is given to the organisation and who in the organisation receives feedback about the sessions?

3. Create a safe environment and establish trust

The coach should provide a safe environment where the coachee feels supported. To effectively establish trust and intimacy, the coach should demonstrate a non-judgemental disposition and unconditional positive regard. Unconditional positive regard means that the person is inherently worthy, regardless of accomplishments or behaviour. The coach should appreciate and respect the coachee's experience and work with the coachee to develop physical and psychological conditions for growth.

'No one can make a plant grow, but if someone were to provide the right conditions, water, nutrients, and soil, it becomes the best plant it can be.' (Tolan, 2003).

At the start of the coaching session, there are some fundamental steps a coach should take to establish trust and intimacy. These steps are known as CPR (Confidentiality, Permission, and Responsibility). The coach should provide a definition of coaching, and explain that a collaborative coach does not offer advice or solutions; the coachee is responsible for any actions taken as a result of the coaching session. At this point, the coach should also explain that the conversation is confidential between the coach and coachee. The coach should also explain that the coachee has permission not to answer any questions that they do not want to answer. An example of this may be relevant where a coachee feels that answering a question may lead to a breach of confidentiality in relation to a work situation or where a coachee may be sensitive and not willing to discuss some aspect of their life.

This conversation may begin as follows:

'Before we discuss what goal or outcome you would like to get from today's session, I would like to clarify some basic contexts of the coaching session. All information discussed between us is confidential. As collaborative coaching is a non-directive process, any decisions you make or actions you take are your responsibility. If there is something you prefer not to discuss or explore, please tell me and we can agree to move on.'

4. Manage the Coaching Process including use of models and techniques and Create Awareness

The structure of the coaching process is such that the coach manages the coaching process i.e., uses a coaching model such as the ARCH model (the acronym ARCH means Achieve, Relevant, Choices, Headway and is discussed further later in the book), whereas the coachee is responsible for creating the agenda. The coach should be adaptable and flexible with the coachee's agenda, be able to step into the coachee's shoes and 'meet the coachee where they are at'. The coach may bring a presence that includes humour, motivation, leadership, and encouragement to the session. The coach should be comfortable responding to strong emotions while maintaining personal emotional self-management. The coach is skilled in both supporting and provoking the coachee to seek alternative options and solutions. In keeping with a non-judgemental approach, a coach should be able to manage their own emotions and personal biases. The coach should be fully present to the coachee and act like a GPS or satellite system that maps out a structure and roadmap for managing the coaching process.

The coach supports the coachee in developing self-awareness and in understanding the impact they have on others. The coach works with the coachee to see other people's perspectives – the difference between their interpretation and the facts. A coach will challenge the coachee on their thoughts, feelings, beliefs, and assumptions. The coach works with the coachee to illuminate gaps and contradictions between behaviour and aspirations to help prioritise goals. In this collaborative process, the coach will express insights and give feedback to identify what is working and what is not working in the current situation.

5. Demonstrate Active Listening Skills

Active listening is a core skill of successful coaching. Active listening is a combination of communication techniques such as paraphrasing, reflecting, summarising, and reframing. It also necessitates being curious and focused on listening – listening to what is not being said as much as to what is being said. In the process of active listening, the coach learns about the coachee's values and beliefs and builds on the coachee's ideas and suggestions. Most people listen to confirm what they think they know and filter out all of the rest; they listen to agree and to disagree with the speaker – this is not active listening.

6. Effective and Powerful Questioning Skills

Effective questioning skills reveal the coachee to themselves; they build self-awareness and help to clarify emotions, values and motivations. The coach uses open questioning techniques to evoke discovery, insight, and commitment to action. Powerful questioning techniques bring the coachee to a deeper level of understanding. They support a coachee to consider at a deeper level the causes and reasons for different behaviours, thoughts, and feelings.

7. Clear and Direct Communication

The coach uses clear, direct, and respectful language, allows the conversation to flow and avoids giving advice, leading, or offering solutions. The coach adapts a communication style that reflects and supports the coachee's communication style, and manages their own emotions to avoid bringing personal judgements and biases into the conversation. The coach provides feedback on what they are picking up and sensing during the session, and supports the coachee in understanding different perspectives.

8. Facilitate Growth and Co-design Action Plans

- Co-designing actions

The coach works with the coachee to increase the coachee's self-awareness in areas such as their own perceptions; reality and assumption; and their interpretation of events. The coach works with the coachee to co-create opportunities for ongoing learning. The coach will work with the coachee to define actions that will enable the coachee to demonstrate, practise, and deepen new learning. Together they systematically explore specific concerns, alternative solutions and options that are central to agreed-upon coaching goals. The coach promotes active experimentation and self-discovery and supports the coachee in setting realistic but stretching goals and outcomes.

- Planning and goal setting

The coach and coachee create a plan with results that are specific, measurable, achievable, realistic, and include an agreed timeline. These goals may be adjusted depending on changing situations and contexts. The coach encourages the coachee to celebrate success at each milestone and to push through resistance and setbacks. The coach helps the coachee to recognise their skills and tools and acknowledge that they have achieved and created success in the past and can continue to create success in the future.

9. Manage Progress and Accountability

- The coach collaborates with the coachee to monitor goal achievement, holds the coachee responsible and accountable for goals agreed, and supports the coachee in staying on track and reviewing agreed goals.

- The coach holds attention on what is important for the client while leaving responsibility with the client to take action. The coach is flexible in adjusting to and working with the coachee on the coachee's agenda.

- The coach demonstrates an ability to simultaneously move back and forth between the current context and long-term goals.

- In addition to monitoring goal commitment, the coach works with the coachee to deepen the learning and reflect on both successes and setbacks.

- The coach prepares and maintains appropriate records, and organises and reviews client information obtained during sessions. The coach also promotes the coachee's self-discipline and develops the coachee's ability to make decisions, address key concerns, determine priorities, and set the pace of learning.

The competencies listed above form the backbone of a successful coaching relationship and will be discussed in further detail later in the book.

Reflective Exercise

Working with the competencies listed, reflect on your current level of skill in these areas. The competencies are listed below with a scale. During your reflective exercise consider on a scale of one to ten, where one indicates a low level and ten indicates a high level of competency, where you would rank yourself on each of these competencies.

Coaching Competencies Schedule

Present a Professional Image	1 _____5_____10
Setting the Coaching Agreement	1 _____5_____10
Create a Safe Environment and Establish Trust	1 _____5_____10
Manage the Coaching Process including the use of models and techniques and Create Awareness	1 _____5_____10
Demonstrate Active Listening	1 _____5_____10
Effective and Powerful Questioning Skills	1 _____5_____10
Clear and Direct Communication	1 _____5_____10
Facilitate Growth and Co-Design Action Plans	1 _____5_____10
Manage Progress & Accountability	1 _____5_____10

Above competencies are based on Professional coaching associations' competency guidelines including the EMCC (European Mentoring & Coaching Council), IAPC&M (International Authority for Professional Coaching & Mentors), the ICF (International Coaching Federation), and the AC (Association for Coaching)

Reflective Exercise

As a starting point for your skills development and based on the results from the above schedule, note in the Strengths Goals Competency Box one: Strengths that you will continue to further develop, and note in the Development Needs Goals Competency box two: Development Needs that you will commit to improving. You can then review these periodically as you develop and grow your skills.

Strengths Competencies

Write TEXT Here

Development Opportunities

Write TEXT Here

What makes a good coach?

Now that we have examined coaching definitions and competencies, let us consider what makes a great coach.

There are some qualities that immediately come to mind:

- Excellent communication skills
- Powerful questioning ability to clarify issues for the benefit of both coachee and coach
- Great coaches have the ability to build trust and demonstrate that they are honourable and credible
- Being neutral and non-judgemental
- Being able to inspire and motivate
- Ability to act as co-pilot to the coachee. They collaborate with the coachee so that the coachee reaches a successful destination
- They help the coachee connect to those big-picture goals e.g. organisation's needs vs personal needs
- They demonstrate empathy. They understand coachee's feelings about what they need to do and their role in the story
- They are comfortable with challenging the coachee and exploring different perspectives

Indicators to a successful outcome are:

- Does the coachee feel better for having spent time with the coach?
- Would the coachee's life be less enriched if they had not met the coach?

A collaborative coach runs the coaching process, understands the coachee's needs and that the coachee has the resources and inner knowledge to find the correct solution. Acting as a GPS system, the collaborative coach guides and supports the coachee in exploring solutions, and is able to step into and understand the coachee's world.

What is important to a coachee when they are looking for a coach?

- Rapport – all the skills and tools will not achieve a successful outcome if rapport is not established and maintained
- Trust
- Respect
- Availability to meet
- How the coach has developed their expertise and continues to expand their knowledge
- How effective the coach is in establishing:
    - Objectivity
    - An ability to provide a safe place to talk

- - An ability to empathise while challenging and asking provocative questions
- Ability of the coach to:
  - Co-design with the coachee goals that are specific, relevant, and achievable
  - Develop new skills and knowledge
  - Inspire and help the coachee when the going gets tough
  - Motivate and enthuse
  - Celebrate and be proud of coachee's success and progress

Chapter 2: Coaching in the Workplace

'Coaching is unlocking people's potential to maximize their own performance. It is more often helping them to learn rather than teaching them' John Whitmore, Executive Coach and Author

Introduction

In this chapter you will:

- Define executive and business coaching
- Examine the difference between executive/business coaching and life coaching
- Consider the language and culture of the business environment
- Understand the coaching contract
- Explore what makes a good executive coach
- Examine additional coaching tools
- Discuss the role of manager as coach

Definition of Executive Coaching

> 'Helping leaders get unstuck from their dilemmas and assisting them in transferring their learning into results for the organisation'
> – (O'Neill, 2013)

Businesses today are faced with ongoing disruption and change. In today's fast paced, Volatile, Uncertain, Complex, and Ambiguous (VUCA) environment, executives and businesses have to manage day-to-day affairs while anticipating rapidly changing marketplace demands. Increasingly, companies and executives are turning to coaches for support to navigate these demands. A collaborative coaching approach enables organisations and executives to capitalise on their own internal resources to find solutions to the challenges they face. The focus on coaching in the workplace in this book is to introduce you to some fundamentals of business/executive coaching. The second book in this series will focus further on coaching in the workplace.

Business and Executive Coaching

Business and executive coaching is a collaborative process that helps an organisation, through its people, to develop more rapidly and produce better results. It can be applied to all types of businesses, from large corporations, government and public service bodies, and small to medium-size enterprises (SMEs).

Business/executive coaching sessions are often linked to specific initiatives or objectives in an organisation or a division of the organisation. Such objectives include Change Management, Sales Enhancement, Career Management, Leadership, Development, Establishing Direction, Vision and Results, Planning/Budgeting, and Organising Resources.

Business/executive coaching is oriented towards results – with a focus on developing improved performance to achieve better results, and profit and return on investment for the organisation. The coach supports managers to operationalise goals, clarify strategy, and build plans. It can be applied to all types of businesses, large corporations, government and public service bodies, down to SMEs.

At an organisational level, a coaching programme can help to address a range of challenges such as staff retention, building leadership, communications enhancement, increasing productivity or sales, improving customer satisfaction, achieving new strategic objectives, career path development and choices, capability to manage stress or avoid derailment, and behavioural or even cultural change.

Business/executive coaches are often called in when a business is perceived to be performing badly, but many businesses recognise the benefits of business coaching even when the organisation is successful.

A Business/Executive coach will often take a multifaceted approach to helping a business improve.

- In some cases, a top-down approach is needed; such as when a CEO with control issues is hindering the success of the company
- In other cases, a bottom-up approach is required, working with a team or individual employees to better understand their potential

Executive coaching is a facet of the business coaching industry and the two terms tend to be used interchangeably.

Executive coaching is a facilitative three-way partnership between the executive, the coach, and the organisation, in which all involved agree on specific goals and parameters.

The focus of the coaching is organisational objectives; it addresses how the personal component impacts on this.

The results produced from this relationship are observable and measurable, commensurate with the requirements the organisation has for the performance of the person being coached.

Reflective Exercise

Consider and reflect on the following statement: A good business coach need not have specific business expertise or experience in the same field as the person receiving the coaching, in order to provide good business coaching.

Differences/similarities between Business/Executive coaching and Life coaching

There are both differences and similarities between business/executive coaching and life coaching.

Similarities include core coaching skills as discussed in Core Coaching Competencies (see section on Introduction to Coaching). However, differences may arise in the themes raised during business/executive coaching sessions.

Business/executive coaching themes:

1. Skills and performance

    o Learn a new skill/grow a capability
    o Solve a problem
    o Make an important business decision
    o Adapt management style/make a behavioural change
    o Improve personal/professional performance

2. Leadership

    - Explore what is happening now, what is the current reality
    - Prepare for a future leadership role, develop vision. What are the trends? What is emerging?
    - Become a more effective leader, explore how the leader sustains themselves
    - Manage organisational change
    - Develop your influencing skills
    - Become more strategic, develop goals direction and outputs
    - Build a higher performing team and organisation, cultivate growth, courage, and capacity for action despite uncertainty and constant change
    - Get support during a difficult time, manage anxiety, filter, understand and diffuse blocks to energy
    - Clarify insights and help the leader leverage their intuitions and insights into actions for the good of the organisation

3. Professional development

    - Get closure around some unfinished business affecting your work e.g. a conflict in a working relationship
    - Improve your self-regulation
    - Develop your emotional intelligence
    - Develop deeper self-belief and confidence
    - Deal with personal change/transition
    - Career progression
    - Behavioural change
    - Find greater meaning, satisfaction, and balance in life and work
    - Make a major life change

In addition, business language and terminology may be different to language used in life coaching. Organisational language may include a focus on words such as data, methodologies, action plans, outcomes, and metrics.

A coach is not expected to be an expert in the industry sector or have in-depth knowledge of the organisation in which they are working. However, it is of benefit if the coach can understand the business world and can demonstrate the benefits of coaching to the particular organisation/company.

The coach should have insight into the challenges faced by the organisation and the department to which the coachee is attached and the stage of development of the organisation. In addition, during the chemistry session, the coach should gain an understanding of the skills and competencies required by the individual to be successful. Depending on the focus of the sessions, understanding the coachee's strengths and development opportunities may be relevant.

Notwithstanding technological advances and the evolution of artificial intelligence, there are many areas in which human input continues to play an important role. The executive coach can work with the coachee to focus on the human skills necessary to create success in this changing environment. Such areas include understanding behaviours, motivating and creating trusting, working relationships with both individuals and teams. Executive coaches can support workers and leaders to develop these necessary skills. Whereas technology and artificial intelligence can solve complex problems and offer solutions, it takes an emotionally intelligent and aware human being to encourage, support, develop and manage tensions, and boost morale. The executive coach can support coachees in the role of developing these skills to create success using increasingly advanced artificial intelligence and technological techniques.

Organisation's and coachee's needs

The diagram below shows the relationship between the organisation's needs and the coachee's needs and may prompt exploration based on the following questions:

- What is the purpose of the organisation?
- What are the needs of the organisation?
- What is the coachee's purpose?
- What are the needs of the coachee?
- How can both the organisation's and coachee's needs be aligned?
- What opportunity for enhanced performance and return on investment for the organisation, and fulfilment for the coachee, can be created with this shared alignment?

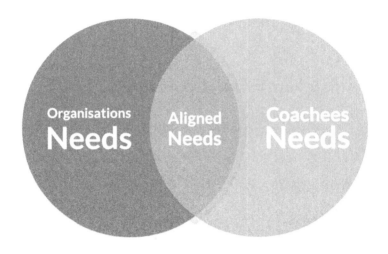

A word of caution to the executive coach. It is important to clarify that the coachee agrees that they want to work with a coach. In some organisations, the coachee may be instructed to work with a coach (called a forced programme) and therefore may be resistant to the coaching process. In the event of a forced programme, establishing trust, assuring confidentiality, and building a collaborative relationship may be the difference between success and failure of the process. Coaching is most effective when the coachee accepts ownership of the coaching programme.

Organisation's Language

A coach may not need to understand the technical intricacies and workings of the industry sector and organisation, however gaining an understanding of the organisation's language is important. Many organisations have abbreviations and three-letter acronyms unique to both their own company and industry. The language used particularly at leadership/managerial level can be indicative of the company's attitude, its level of positivity/negativity, its culture and its value system. Some common business terms and phrases and three-letter acronyms (TLAs) used in the business world are listed in Appendix 1

Coaching & culture of the organisation

A coach needs to be aware of the culture of the company within which he/she is operating. Culture may be described as the personality of the organisation and includes:

- Customs
- Traditions
- Ways of thinking
- Beliefs
- Behaviours

- Style of operating
- Values

The Coaching Contract

A significant difference between Life Coaching and Business/Executive coaching is the Coaching Contract.

The contract is central in the coaching profession in that it sets the professional context for the coach's practice, the client's general objectives (the contracting company), the relationship between the coach, client, and the coachee (the individual who is being coached).

A good contract is clear, specific, and allows all parties to reach a shared understanding of the coaching process. Contracting arrangements for individual and corporate coaching have many similar elements; corporate coaching contracts will contain additional specific information pertaining to the organisation. In the business world, the contract in coaching is often formal and can contain legal overtones. It concerns the general scope of the coach-client relationship. A contract may include the following:

- The goals and desired outcomes for the coaching programme
- The criteria which will be used to measure the success of the programme

- The anticipated length of the programme
- The duration and frequency of coaching sessions
- The fee structure and any cancellation charges
- Agreed processes for cancelling and rescheduling sessions
- The ground rules for the programme:
  - Confidentiality
  - Roles and Responsibilities
  - Boundaries
  - Feedback
  - Taking notes

Arrangements for evaluating the programme

Contracting arrangements for corporate coaching differ from individual contracting in that the purpose of contracting in executive/corporate coaching is to ensure productive outcomes, clarify roles, prevent misunderstandings, establish learning goals, and define business and interpersonal practices.

In corporate coaching contracting there are normally three parties involved in the contract: the coach, the organisation (also known as the client) and the coachee. We call this a multi-handed contract due to the connections between each party. The coach has a contracting relationship with both the client and the coachee. Similarly, the client has a contract with the coach and the coachee and the coachee with both the coach and the client. Each party to the contract should have clarity and transparency with regard to their role, responsibilities, and the outcomes/inputs expected of them in the coaching relationship.

There are three major components of corporate contracting: the Information Contract, the Business/Legal/Financial Contract, and the Coach/Coachee Contract.

The Information Contract includes:

    Aims, purpose and objectives

    Timelines and milestones

    Scope and types of assessment

    Measures of success

    Identification and roles of stakeholders

    Confidentiality agreements

    Guidelines on feedback to client (the hiring authority)

    Guidelines for the use of personal and coaching information

    Guidelines for the communication and distribution of information

Business/Legal/Financial Contracts include:

Executive coaching standards and guidelines

Organisationally sponsored proprietary and confidentiality statements

Guidelines for relevant business practices

Total costs of service: who is paying for coaching services, fee and payment schedules, guidelines for billing procedures, agreements on expense reimbursements

Confirmation of the coach's professional liability insurance

Personal Contracts between the coach and the executive include: Guidelines on honesty, openness, and reliability between executive and coach

Understanding of the coach's theoretical and practical approach and how coaching sessions will be structured

Agreements on scheduling, punctuality, and cancellation of meetings

Scoping of how much pre-work coach and coachee will do before each session

Guidelines on giving and receiving feedback

Understanding of when the coach will be available to the executive and vice versa, and how contact will be made

Agreements on follow-up and documentation

Confirmation of locations and times for meetings and phone calls

Coach/Coachee contract, and the purpose of contracting:

The purpose of contracting is to build trust between the coach and coachee. This is called the psychological contract. The psychological contract is the unspoken agreement between coach and coachee. Successful contracting explores both coach and coachee's expectations, and sets the scene for working together in a collaborative relationship to achieve a win/win for both coach and coachee. If the contracting is not successfully established, the psychological contract may be that the coachee is disappointed when the coach does not give advice and offer solutions. The coachee adopts the mindset 'You are the expert, now fix me'. Ultimately the aim of contracting is to pave the way for a highly rewarding learning experience, where all parties see results and where communication and openness is present throughout.

The role of Human Resources (HR)

Who pays the coach?

The organisation is normally responsible for payment of the coaching services. It is normal practice for the organisation to co-ordinate the selection process.

What is the role of Human Resources?

Human Resources should:

- Provide a list of potential coaches for consideration
- Set up the engagements and agree on the terms and conditions with the coach

HR Commitments: HR plays an integral role in facilitating corporate coaching and contracting. Important behind-the-scenes activities, usually conducted by HR, include sourcing, selecting, and orienting coaches, consulting with executives on their needs, matching coach to executive, and establishing standards for practice.

- HR should facilitate to ensure the best possible experience and outcomes for the executive and the organisation
- Establish and disseminate standards for learning contracts to the coaching organisation and the client organisation

- Actively participate in establishing and supporting the executive's learning contract
- Respect the personal contract as established between the coach and executive
- Ensure that the coach has and uses business/legal/financial contractual information
- Expedite the contracting and payment process in the client organisation in support of the executive and the coach

What makes a good Executive Coach?

In addition to the competencies set out in the Introduction, the Executive Coach should:

Be comfortable with giving challenging and constructive feedback such as 'I agree with you' or 'I disagree with you' and stating the reason

Tune into the relationship at an intuitive level – reflect to the executive about hunches, probe, clarify, and question

Be prepared for resistance

Profile of an executive: The perception gap

In the business world, there is often an assumption that the executive should be strong, independent, and self-reliant. The coach will inevitably come across executives who doubt their own accomplishments and have an internalised fear of being 'found out'. Despite evidence of success, depending on personality type, background, and experiences, this fear can be masked in different ways. Some examples are:

The guilt of success: Feeling not worthy. They keep expecting to feel better as they achieve more and it doesn't happen. With these people, that are drivers, the next achievement is never enough – unless they gain perspective! This is also known as the 'The Imposter Syndrome'.

False bravado & Dress Up: Little boys and girls playing dress-up! Many executives deep down inside feel this way. Executives are clever to make small changes seem big...

The Executive Myth: You think they are one thing and they think another.

Do vs Are: For these executives their egos are completely wrapped up in what they do vs. what they are and what they stand for. A key realisation for them is that their job is not the centre of the universe. Their focus is on status and achievement rather than mission, purpose, and values. They will be driven by task to the detriment of work colleagues, direct reports, peers, and self.

T.F.T.B (Ten Foot Tall and Bulletproof): You will be dealing with people that don't know (consciously) that they need help. Quite the opposite, they will mostly think they are on top of the world. They are ten feet tall and bulletproof. Their mindset is that they have not done and do not need further training, they'll pick it up.

The role of denial: The bigger the ego, the bigger the denial and probably the more they need your help.

Human too: These executives are human just like you and me. They are often full of self-doubt, insecurities, and the sense of not being worthy!

Reflective Exercise:

How often have you come across these various executive profiles?

Case Study:

Michael is the Head of Operations in a medium-sized retail company. He was promoted from his original clerical role through the ranks as the company grew. Although he has some training in management skills, he believes that the best training comes through experience and he is intelligent enough to read his environment. He has always been a keen and enthusiastic individual who constantly delivered excellent results and has been concerned that employees don't appear to share his drive and enthusiasm.

Recently he was shocked when the CEO told him that despite his often-enthusiastic disposition, employees found that on occasions he was moody and difficult, particularly when he was under pressure and stressed. He seemed to withdraw and resort to the silent treatment when confronted with setbacks. His behaviour impacted the atmosphere in the office and on the floor.

I was approached by the CEO to work with Michael. Michael's story is not unusual, his variety of being 'Ten Foot Tall and Bulletproof' was underpinned by his denial of the need to change. Through the use of a 360-degree feedback assessment where anonymous feedback was given to Michael by direct reports and peers on his behaviour, Michael saw evidence of how he was perceived by others. Over a period of six months, I worked with Michael and explored his behaviours and how they were triggered. In a collaborative coaching process, we put in place a plan of ongoing development to become aware of and change his mindset, judgements, and assumptions. As with any coaching intervention, the starting point is for the coachee to acknowledge the gap between how they see themselves, their level of self-awareness, and how others experience their behaviours. In a collaborative coaching process, closing this perception gap can bring long term lasting benefits.

Strategic analysis the IGOR (Internal Capability, Gap, Opportunities, Risks) acronym

Whereas the business/executive coach does not need to have industry expertise, it is of benefit for the coach to have an understanding of the basic principles of strategic planning. The coach can support the coachee in the tactical implementation of the desired strategy. One such method is to explore the organisation's or executive's strengths and development needs and from this formulate a strategic plan to move forward.

As a coach, work with the coachee to identify:

Internal Capability

What does the business or executive do well?

In what areas are they successful?

Gap

What are the internal or external processes or behaviours that are a block to success?

Opportunities

What are the areas or behaviours in which the business or executive can improve performance?

Risks

What are the factors that might inhibit the growth or development of the business or executive?

Another process that can be used in coaching (both business and life coaching) is a cost-benefit analysis (CBA). During a coaching conversation, the coach will work with the coachee to assess the benefits of a particular action or decision and then evaluate the costs or drawbacks. This can be further explored in the context of the opportunity cost i.e. what are the alternative courses of action or options that will be missed as a result of selecting the current one that is being analysed.

Case Study:

Jonathan had twenty years' experience working in a large marketing, design, and consulting company. In a recent meeting with his manager, Jonathan was told that he would be made redundant from his role as a Team Lead and senior graphics designer. With the benefit of a significant cash lump sum, he has the option of exploring next steps in his career. Amongst the options he wanted to explore was setting up as an independent consultant. In one of our coaching sessions, we completed a brainstorming exercise to identify topics associated with the subject 'independent consultant' and then completed a cost-benefit analysis of the outcomes. Drawing three columns on a page, we put the following titles in three separate columns, Cost (Disadvantages of being a consultant), Benefit (Advantages of being a consultant) and minus (-) or plus (+) or zero sign in the third column.

If Jonathan considered the topic to be a Cost, he put a (–) in the third column, if it was a benefit, he put a (+) in the third column. The zero sign was used where the costs and benefits negated each other.

Sample of cost-benefit analysis

Cost	Benefit	-, +, 0
Dislike for doing administration tasks	Lack of bureaucracy	0
Risk	Independence	0
Lead-in time to setting up a business	Flexibility in working hours	0
Absence of working with colleagues and support structure	Well established networks	0
Loss of steady income and benefits	Control over charge out rate	0

Inexperienced in selling	Potential personal growth opportunity, comfortable with the challenge	o
Constant juggling between providing core services and administration	None – may lead to increased stress and impact creativity	-
None	Free from organisational politics	+
Loss of work/life balance at the start at start-up phase	None	-
No sense of legacy or long term fulfilment	Have an established business when he reaches retirement age with potential to bring in partner and/or scale back without having to retire fully. Continue to feed his passion	+

At the end of this exercise, the outcome is one that is based on a logical and cognitive-based exploration. It brings clarity to the balance between the Costs and Benefits. The exercise also forms the basis of a deeper dive and exploration into motivations, value systems, work/life balance, and in this case, the bigger agenda of self-actualisation.

The Manager as Coach

Historically, people were promoted within an organisation for their technical skills and their ability to 'hit the ground running and get the job done'. With the popularisation of emotional intelligence, there is an increased awareness of the relevance of people skills in contributing to increased productivity and profitability. Modern day managers engage in ongoing development of self and others and understand the role of coaching skills and also a coaching style of leadership in creating successful outcomes. Intrinsic in this, is cultivating a growth mindset and an environment of psychological safety and trust where people are comfortable with making and learning from mistakes.

In the organizational context, a coach style of management empowers and motivates, invites dialogue, discussion, curiosity, and constructive challenge. Whilst there are times when the manager may have to be directive, the more they use a coaching style, the more they develop autonomy in their teams and direct reports. A coaching style can be used in a two-minute conversation and need not always involve a full coaching session. The key is to work with the person to understand their position and thinking, and encourage them to come up with solutions. This in turn facilitates increased delegation, status, ownership, and a responsibility model, where employees take more ownership of problem solving and decision making. Managers as coaches can exist at all levels within the organization. One of the biggest challenges as a coach manager is balancing the needs of the organization with employee needs.

Case Study

Mary is the manager of her department in a medium sized company. It is common knowledge in the organisation that she will retire in three years. She has been asked by the head of her business unit to get involved in a significant but highly confidential project that will start in the next two months. Mary is keen to get involved in the new project.

Paul is the highest performer on her team and she has identified him as her successor when she retires. Mary is aware that Paul is currently frustrated and is keen to get promoted. He has been very open with her and explained that he enjoys working in the company. However, he is not willing to hang around for her to retire in order to gain promotion. To this end he has begun to look for opportunities outside of the company.

In order for Mary to accept her role on the new project, she will have to either 'hold on to' Paul or recruit externally to find a suitable replacement to fill the role. The role is a very specialised one and finding and, given the tight timeline, on-boarding someone new will be very difficult. Mary likes to engage in a coaching style of management and seeks when at all possible, to meet the needs of both the organisation and her employees. She is conflicted about how to manage this situation and retain Paul without compromising confidentiality in relation to the new role.

In adopting a coaching role, Mary first of all agreed that their conversation would be confidential between them. She wanted to ensure that their conversation was held in a psychologically secure environment where it was safe for them to express their thoughts and feelings. She told Paul that she was aware of his thoughts with regards to next steps in his career. In keeping with a coaching style, she suggested that she hoped the outcome (goal) from their conversation would be to find some sort of agreeable solution for both him and the organisation. She emphasised that he played a key role in the company and that his expertise and ability was widely acknowledged. Whilst she was unable to share with him anything about the forthcoming project, she enquired from him what his greatest fears were about remaining in his current role in the organisation. He explained that he felt waiting until she retired to improve his level of responsibility and earnings would undermine all the effort he had put into developing himself and his career progression to date. Already he was aware of his colleagues in other organisations progressing to the next level and being rewarded for their commitment and dedication.

Through Mary's opening questioning techniques, Paul realized that he was, in truth, sitting on the fence about leaving the organisation. He acknowledged that the company invested heavily in developing staff, acknowledged hard work, and rewarded performance through small but meaningful gestures such as gift vouchers, annual leave above the norm, early finish times on Fridays and respecting the need for a healthy work life balance. Having established that he was not completely committed to leaving the company, she then did a brainstorm exercise with him to look at ways of motivating him to stay. One of the outcomes was an increase in responsibility and with that some financial recognition.

When wrapping up and concluding the conversation, they agreed that Paul would keep Mary updated on potential opportunities as they arose outside of the organisation. Mary in turn said that she would explore all avenues in relation to increasing his level of responsibility and keep him updated on progress on this matter.

SUMMARY

Whether you are involved in coaching in the business environment or in life coaching, the basic foundation coaching skills are the same. Ongoing learning into human development and behaviours and how they impact are pivotal to achieving enduring, successful, and lasting success both as a coach and leader. This ongoing learning, combined with a coach developing their own unique style where they combine skills, tools, competencies, self-management, and self-awareness, is the hallmark of effective coaching.

People come to coaching because they want to change something; it inevitably leads to a change in self-awareness, a realisation that they have blind spots, habits that sabotage performance and that are not effective. They look to the services of a coach to support them in making this change.

Chapter 3: The Coaching Process – How to Develop Coaching Skills and Competencies

> 'I suppose it is tempting, if the only tool you have is a hammer, to treat everything as if it were a nail' Abraham Maslow, psychologist

Introduction

In this chapter you will:

- Discuss learning styles
- Discuss the collaborative coaching mindset
- Learn about questioning skills

Understanding How People Learn

What is the connection between how people learn and coaching?

The more a coach understands how a person processes information and how they experience the world, the better the coach is able to 'step into that person's world'. Similarly, the more a coachee understands how they process information and experience their world, the more they develop self-awareness and also an understanding of the differences between themselves and other people they interact with. This awareness is relevant both in life coaching and also in the corporate context where we are continuously working with a wide range of people.

David Kolb's Experiential Learning Theory model

David A. Kolb's learning model is based on the Experiential Learning Theory (ELT), as explained in his book *Experiential Learning* (Kolb & Fry, 1974).

The ELT model outlines two related approaches towards *grasping* experience – **Concrete Experience** and **Abstract Conceptualisation** – as well as two related approaches towards *transforming* experience: **Reflective Observation** and **Active Experimentation**. According to Kolb's model, the ideal learning process engages all four of these modes in response to situational demands. In order for learning to be effective, all four of these approaches must be incorporated. As individuals attempt to use all four approaches, however, they tend to develop strengths in one experience-grasping approach and one experience-transforming approach.

In my training courses I describe four styles based on Kolb's model that relate to managerial experiences of decision making/problem-solving. The four styles are:

- The Realist (Concrete Experience)
- The Intellectual (Abstract Conceptualisation)
- The Observer (Reflective Observer)
- The Doer (Active Experimentation)

A coach should understand and recognise their main learning style(s) and be aware that they will tend to have a preference for one or two learning styles over the others and understand the impact this may have on their coaching style. In turn, the coach should work with the coachee to support them in understanding their learning style(s) and the impact this may have on their interactions with others – be it in a managerial or personal context.

In addition, the coach should support the coachee to:

- Become aware of others' learning styles and learn to adapt their styles and so work more effectively with others
- Become familiar with their learning style(s) and therefore be in a far better position to do three things:

1. Make their learning easier, more effective and more enjoyable. The coachee becomes smarter at getting a better fit between learning opportunities and the way they learn best. It saves them tackling your learning on a hit-and-miss basis.

2. Become more aware of and adaptable in their learning style especially when working with others with different styles. The skill of adaptability is linked to emotional intelligence. Emotional intelligence leads to greater success both in life and in the workplace. Becoming an all-round learner increases your versatility and helps you learn from a wide variety of different experiences – some formal, some informal, some planned and some spontaneous.

3. Improves their learning skills and processes. Increased awareness of how they learn opens up the whole process to self-scrutiny and improvement. Learning to learn is an important capability since it provides the gateway to everything else you want to develop.

The Doer:

The Doer learns by action. They have an open-minded approach to learning, involving themselves fully and without bias in new experiences. They prefer to get their hands dirty and to learn by experience. They prefer learning activities that include:

- Creative brainstorming
- Group discussion
- Puzzles, case-studies, and problem solving
- Competitions
- Role-play

The Doer learns best from activities where:

- There are new experiences/problems/opportunities from which to learn
- They can get involved in short 'here and now' activities such as teamwork tasks or role-playing exercises
- There is excitement or drama and things chop and change with a range of activities to tackle
- They can be in the limelight, such as chairing meetings, leading discussions, or giving presentations
- They are allowed to generate ideas without feeling constrained by policy or practical considerations
- They are thrown in at the deep end with a challenging task or in adverse conditions

- They are involved with other people
- They feel free to 'have a go'

The Doer learns least from, and may react against activities where:

- Learning involves a passive role
- They have to stand back and not be involved
- They have to process a lot of data
- They have to work a lot on their own
- They have to identify beforehand what it is they will learn, and assess afterwards what they have learned
- They are given a lot of what they regard as theory
- They have to repeat an activity frequently
- They have to follow very detailed instructions with little room for initiative
- They have to attend to detail

The Realist:

These people need to be able to see how to put the learning into practice in the real world. Abstract concepts and games are of limited use unless they can see a way to put the ideas into action in their lives. They learn best from experimenting, trying out new ideas, theories, and techniques to see if they work. They prefer learning activities that include:

- Time to think about how to apply learning in reality
- Case studies
- Problem-solving
- Discussion

Realists learn best from activities where:

- There is an obvious link between the subject matter and a problem or opportunity on the job
- They are shown techniques for doing things with obvious practical advantages, such as how to save time
- They have the chance to try out and practise techniques with coaching or feedback from a credible expert
- They are exposed to a model they can copy, such as a respected mentor
- They are given techniques currently applicable to their own job
- The learning activity is deemed to be valid, i.e. has relevance or applicability in the real world
- They can concentrate on practical issues, for example, drawing up action plans

Realists learn least from, and may react against activities where:

- The learning is not related to an immediate need they recognise, i.e. when it is perceived to be abstract
- Organisers of the learning, or the event itself, seems distant from reality
- There is no clear set of guidelines on how to do it
- They feel that people are going round in circles and not getting anywhere
- There are political, managerial, or personal obstacles to applying the learning

The Intellectual:

These learners like to understand the theory behind the actions. They need models, concepts, and facts in order to engage in the learning process. They prefer to analyse and synthesise, drawing new information into a systematic and logical 'theory'. They prefer learning activities that include:

- Models
- Statistics
- Stories
- Quotes

- Background information
- Applying theories

Intellectuals learn best from activities where:

- What is being offered is part of a system, model concept, or theory
- They have time to explore methodically the associations and interrelationships between ideas, events, and situations
- They have the chance to question the basic method, assumptions, or logic behind something
- They are intellectually stretched
- They are in structured situations with a clear purpose
- They can listen to or read about ideas or concepts that emphasise rationality or logic that are well-argued or elegant
- They can analyse and then generalise the reasons for success or failure
- They are offered interesting ideas and concepts even though they are not immediately relevant
- They are required to understand and participate in complex situations

Intellectuals learn least from, and may react against activities where:

- They are pitched into doing something without knowing the context or apparent purpose
- They have to participate in situations emphasising emotions and feelings
- They are involved in unstructured activities where ambiguity and uncertainty are high
- They are asked to act or decide without a basis in policy, principle, or concept
- They are faced with a hotchpotch of alternative or contradictory methods without exploring any in depth
- They doubt that the subject matter is methodologically sound, for example, where there aren't any statistics to support an argument
- They find the subject matter shallow or gimmicky
- They feel themselves out of tune with other participants, i.e. when with lots of doers and people who like action.

The Observer:

These people learn by observing, tend to be thinkers, and need time and space to reflect about the situation. They may avoid leaping in and prefer to stand back, watch and view experiences from a number of different perspectives, collecting data and taking the time to work towards an appropriate conclusion. They prefer learning activities that include:

- Paired discussions
- Self-analysis questionnaires
- Personality questionnaires
- Time out
- Observing activities
- Feedback from others
- Coaching
- Interviews

Observers learn best from activities where:

- They are allowed or encouraged to watch or think over activities
- They are able to stand back from events and observe or listen
- They are allowed to think before acting or commenting, or have time to prepare
- They can carry out some painstaking research
- They have the opportunity to review what has happened or review what they have learned

- They are asked to produce carefully considered reports
- They can exchange views with other people in safety
- They can reach a decision in their own time without pressure and tight deadlines

Observers learn least from, and may react against activities where:

- They feel forced into the limelight
- They are involved in situations which require action without planning
- They are pitched into doing something without warning and feel put on the spot
- They are given insufficient information on which to assess a situation
- They are given cut and dried instructions on how things should be done
- They are worried about time pressures
- They have to take short cuts or do a superficial job

Case Study:

I was delivering an executive coach training programme to a group of managers in an organisation. As part of the training, I was demonstrating a coaching session to the participants. The person I was coaching had an Observer learning style. The other course participants sat, watched, and listened to how the session unfolded.

I knew that to be effective, build rapport, and develop a relationship with the coachee, I needed to match his Observer's style and move at his cadence during the session. There were many silences and pauses while I allowed the coachee to process the different questions I asked, and allowed him to think, formulate answers, consider, and reconsider his own answers.

I was working patiently and respectfully with the coachee when I heard one of the 'watchers' of the session comment, 'Would he ever get on with it? It's like watching paint dry.'

Certainly, there are times when one has to be decisive and move to action. However, it is when we are unable to value and respect the different needs in others' communication styles that relationships break down. The judgements that we carry in our heads influence the impact we have when communicating with others. Of course, equally, the individual with an Observer learning style needs to be aware of the needs of the fast-paced Doer. However, it is the role of managers and leaders to adapt their style, to nurture, and bring their teams along with them.

Reflective Exercise

Consider the above styles, based on your self-awareness and personal insight which of the styles above most represents your learning style?

What is the relevance of learning styles from a coaching perspective?

It is important to be aware of your own learning style. Although you will have qualities from each style, it is probable that you may have a preference for one or two learning styles more than the others. It is also important to have awareness of the coachee's style. Through asking open questions and learning about these different styles, a coach develops an intuitive insight to a coachee's learning style.

What does the coach need to be aware of when coaching each style?

The Doer

- The Doer tends to see the big picture and focus on the long-term goals. The coach should work with the Doer to break a goal down into small pictures/milestones and plan a goal built on a step-by-step basis
- It is important to get the coachee to commit to a time frame

- What challenges do they envisage? Doers like to think of challenges but need to be held to account. Ask the coachee if a plan doesn't work what they would do differently

- Doers like role-play, brainstorming, puzzles, problem-solving

- They can be forgetful and therefore they like someone to check in with them and support/motivate them (they tend to be extrinsically motivated, so collaboration with and support from others is important)

- Find out who their key stakeholders are and who will support them after coaching is complete

The Realist

- The Realist will ask, 'Who else do you know who has done this, achieved this goal?' and copy steps from another person

- Make a plan based on a model

- Will ask 'Who can I get the expertise from?'

- What is the process required – and break the process into small steps

- Long term goal needs clarity – start with the outcome and work back – can be good project managers

- Goals and outcomes must be relevant to life. Practical application is important – clear understanding of next step
- They need action
- They can be impatient and dismissive
- They tend to like to work in a quick and efficient manner
- A Realist prefers to 'further the action, rather than deepen the learning'

The Intellectual

The Intellectual will ask, 'What do I need to carry out this goal?', 'What is the process I need to go through or develop to achieve this goal?'

- Intellectuals like clearly defined action plans and clearly defined goals
- They look for evidence of success through a role model and tend to be more cautious rather than risk-takers
- They like an evidence-based, logical, analytical approach
- They tend to like concrete decision making – when a decision is made it is made
- Too many questions may frustrate them – they like time to think and weigh up options

The Observer

- The Observer thinks and analyses

- They can procrastinate and see obstacles!

- Detail is important and therefore Observers tend to take time when making decisions and therefore don't like to be timebound – the coach can challenge an Observer and ask 'what might happen if you let go of the need to pay attention to detail?'

- Doesn't like to be put under pressure

- Needs time to reflect, analyse and think, and so the session may be quite slow-paced

- They need to process and not be rushed. It is important that they feel listened to

- Remember as a coach to adapt your language pace to the coachee's style

- In addition to understanding the coachee's style, the coach also needs to be aware of his/her own style and pace of working

Reflective Exercise

As coach who has a Doer learning style, what do you need to be aware of when coaching

      An Observer Style?

An Intellectual Style?

A Realist Style?

As coach who has an Intellectual learning style, what do you need to be aware of when coaching

An Observer Style?

A Doer Style?

A Realist Style

As coach who has a Realist learning style, what do you need to be aware of when coaching

An Observer Style?

An Intellectual Style?

A Doer Style?

As coach who has an Observer learning style, what do you need to be aware of when coaching

A Doer Style?

An Intellectual Style?

A Realist Style?

Collaborative coaching

Collaboration takes place when we park our own personal biases and judgements. Barriers to collaboration exist when we believe that our thoughts, ideas, and beliefs are correct and that life should be lived according to our rules. Research suggests the average person has 60,000 thoughts a day. We repeat 90% to 95% of those thoughts every day (Dispenza, 2014). We carry with us a narrative about how the world works; we struggle with accommodating others' opinions and view of the world and are locked into our own belief systems, biases, and mindsets. Collaborative coaching is a mindset that underpins all coaching conversations.

In collaborative coaching both the coach and the coachee engage in an adult-to-adult relationship. The coach recognises that the coachee is a capable, resourceful, and creative person. The coach supports the coachee to find solutions, explore learnings from setbacks and disappointments, recognise emotional responses, and examine behavioural patterns. The success of the collaborative coach lies in their ability to support, inspire, motivate, and empower the coachee.

The collaborative coach, therefore, adopts a non-judgemental mindset of unconditional positive regard where the coachee

is free to explore, speak and share thoughts, emotions, successes and setbacks in a safe and trusted environment.

In collaborative coaching, success for the coachee is achieved through the coach:

- Managing self-awareness
- Being non-judgemental
- Engaging in Active Listening
- Using elucidation and clarification of context and situation
- Inspiring the coachee to action, being creative and resourceful
- Displaying commitment to supporting coachee's growth and change

The Collaborative Coaching Mindset

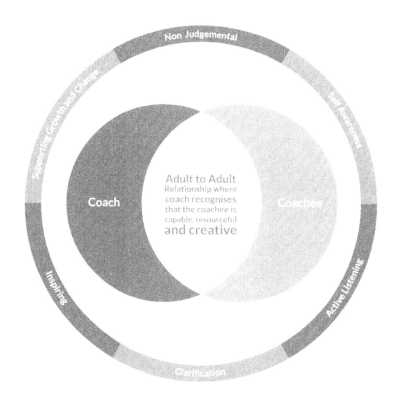

Questioning Skills

Rogers (2012) – 'If you genuinely believe in the resourcefulness of your clients, you have to find alternative ways to giving advice'.

Questioning

Coaching is about asking incisive questions rather than providing solutions. The coachee may never have asked themselves these questions before, for various reasons and they will benefit enormously from addressing them. The art of skilful questioning is one of the most important competencies in coaching and the use of open questions is very powerful. By asking open questions, the coach supports the coachee in becoming more self-aware. Through a combination of skilful questioning, listening skills, curiosity, and interpreting nonverbal body language signals, the coach can access their intuition and can reflect and summarise to the coachee key insights arising from the conversations. Collaborative coaching is about creating awareness rather than offering solutions or advice and, as such, is a specifically non-directive intervention. Therefore, questioning is very important in the coaching relationship, and it is particularly important that a coach knows how to ask effective questions. Different types of questions are discussed later in this chapter.

Definition of a question

- The action of enquiring or asking; the stating or investigation of a problem; to inquire or seek after.

Definition of an effective question

- An effective question is a question that involves the seeking of information which in turn directs towards further understanding. It is like a key that unlocks a door and opens up endless possibilities.

What is the purpose of questioning in a collaborative coaching conversation?

Questioning in the coaching context enables the coach to:

- Gather information
- Develop rapport
- Establish a relationship between coach and client
- Build trust through acceptance
- Encourage client

- To explore
- To think
- To be creative
- Empower coachee
- To change the way of thinking
- To explore different perspectives
- Motivate the client
- To come up with the answers
- Clarify the real issue
- 'Push buttons' and help the coachee identify their real feelings about the challenge; this may lead to deeper insights, self-awareness and understanding
- Help coachee explore limiting beliefs and assumptions
- Help coachee reflect and hear what they need to hear
- Keep a coachee focused

What are the best questions?

If the coach asks open questions, there are no wrong or right questions. However, the coach should:

- Listen without judgement (otherwise the client may tell you what they think you want to hear)
- Avoid anticipating the answer (avoid leading the coachee and, therefore, ensure the coachee gets the right answer for himself/herself)
- Avoid giving advice

Ask open questions. What is the reason for asking open questions?

'Telling or asking closed questions saves a person from having to think. Asking open questions causes them to think for themselves' – *Sir John Whitmore, Coaching for Performance,* (Whitmore, 2009)

Open questions, i.e. questions such as

- Who…?
- What…?
- When…?
- Where…?

- How...?

An open question can generate and encourage the coachee to explore a number of possible solutions. This will give more information and expand the conversation. For example:

- A 'Did...?' question usually elicits a 'Yes' or 'No' answer.
- A 'What...?' question can be useful to get a client to see different perspectives.
- Changing 'Why...?' to 'What...?'

Why questions - a coachee may feel judged if a question is phrased 'why did you do that?' – be careful how they are used. Think back to your childhood, what question did an adult ask you when you did something wrong? Cultivate a habit of changing *why* questions to *what* questions.

Why did you do that?

To

What was the benefit of doing that?

What was the reason for doing that?

Questions that ask, 'What...?' help a person to stay grounded in the present moment. Questions that ask, 'Why...?', in addition to leading a person into emotions, justifying, and explaining, also take a person out of the present moment. According to Peter Bluckett (Bluckett,

2008), an increase in self-awareness is based on what is happening for us in the present moment. When working with a coachee on developing self-awareness and self-understanding, a coach might encourage a coachee to ask themselves, 'What is happening right now? What are you thinking? What are you feeling? What do you notice in yourself? What do you want right now?' All these questions are in the present tense and are likely to create greater understanding of immediate thoughts, feelings, and needs. These direct types of questions may cause discomfort in a coachee; the coachee may feel as if they are being 'put on the spot'. However, the questions push and challenge the coachee to become more self-aware and to develop greater insight into the 'triggers' that underlie their behaviours and decisions.

Statements such as, 'Tell me more about ...' or, 'I am curious to understand more about this ...' can also be effective in building rapport and gathering information.

What makes a good question?

Good questions are:

- Purposeful – they are asked to achieve a specific purpose
- Clear – the recipient can understand the question
- Brief – stated in as few words as possible

- Simple – stated simply, and in plain English
- Provoking – they stimulate thought and response
- Limited in scope – only one or two points to be considered
- Adapted to suit the level of the recipient. A question posed to children will be different to one posed to an adult.

Types of questions

Clarifying Questions:

These are used to understand the nature, not just the facts, of what the client is sharing. An exception to using open questions is when you are clarifying something. When seeking clarification, we may want a yes or no answer. If you are looking for a yes or no answer the question may start with, 'Is this', as in, 'Is this a want or a need'?

- How important or urgent is this?
- What are you addressing or avoiding?
- What is fact or interpretation?
- How open or resistant are you?
- Is this a want or a need?
- Is this an opportunity or possibility?

- Is this a source or symptom?
- Is this a response or a reaction?
- What are you trying to create vs eliminate?
- Is this a problem or a concern?
- Is this current or past?
- What is not being said?

Being Questions:

- Who are you being right now?
- How proud of yourself are you now?
- Who would you have to be to get through this?
- Who do you remind yourself of?

Integrity Questions:

- What does the word integrity mean to you?
- How important is integrity to you?
- On a scale of one to ten, how true are you to your values?
- How open are you?
- What are you running from?
- What is this really about?

Decision-Making Questions:

- How many big decisions have you already made in your life?
- How did they work out?
- How many decisions do you make every day?
- How do you intend to handle the situation?

Solution Questions:

- How do you intend to handle the situation?
- What one thing could stop you from achieving this solution?
- What if you did nothing at all?
- What question would you ask a person if they were in this situation?
- What is the cleverest way you could solve this?

Encouraging Questions:

- What one benefit will you get from achieving this?
- How will this look in five weeks, five months, five years?
- What vision have you that you are working towards?
- What is another way of looking at this?
- How would you like to be coached on this topic?

Challenging Questions:

- What one thing could you do differently?
- How comfortable are you being challenged by me?
- How soon can you resolve that?
- What is the first step you can take?
- What is possible here?
- What's stopping you?
- What is this really about?
- What's the one change in your life that would make the biggest positive difference?
- How important is it to take back control?
- What are you moving towards or away from?

Some executive coaching questions

Twenty questions

Ask the executive:

How they would describe themselves.

What people see as their strengths and their weaknesses.

How they would describe their company culture.

About their turnover of personnel.

Who are their sounding boards?

If they've ever been blindsided with a business issue.

About comments in exit interviews, when people leave.

About their company's recruiting process.

About the role they play in their company.

What themes continue to come up, repeating patterns?

What is the best thing that playing with their children brings out?

About their last vacation?

How their spouse deals with the pressure of their work.

How they stay in touch with their friends.

What the biggest challenge is that they face at this moment.

What is the weakest part of their company?

How their subordinates would describe them.

How their clients would describe them.

How their competitors would describe them.

How their significant other would describe them.

(Source unknown)

Chapter 4: More About the Coaching Process

'If you want to be happy, set a goal that commands your thoughts, liberates your energy and inspires your hopes'
—Andrew Carnegie

In this chapter you will:

- Learn how to start a coaching session
- Learn and practice a coaching model, the ARCH (Achieve, Relevant, Choices, Headway) model
- Learn about the SMART Model
- Learn how to structure a coaching session
- Understand the importance of goal setting
- Explore how to set 'good' goals

How to start a coaching session

Now that we understand the importance of asking questions in a coaching session, how does a coach start a coaching session?

Each coachee will have a different desired outcome from the coaching. It is important to have a number of different approaches to starting a coaching session. Some people will be structured in the way they approach things, others less so. Below are some approaches that may be worth considering when starting a coaching session.

After establishing the terms and conditions of the coaching agreement and explaining about CPR (Confidentiality, Permission, and Responsibility), as explained in chapter 1 in the section on coaching competencies, one option for starting a coaching conversation is to introduce the coachee to a coaching wheel (See Figs 1 & 2). The coaching wheel helps the coachee in the process of self-discovery, and gives insight into their thoughts and feelings about different areas of their life. The wheel can be co-designed between coach and coachee and can be broken into different segments. By asking the coachee questions, the coach helps the coachee clarify what is working well and what are the gaps and shortfalls that the coachee would like to work on and address.

The diagram below (Fig1) is a simple coaching wheel with four segments: Work, Learning/Growth, Playing, and Giving – a WLPG Wheel.

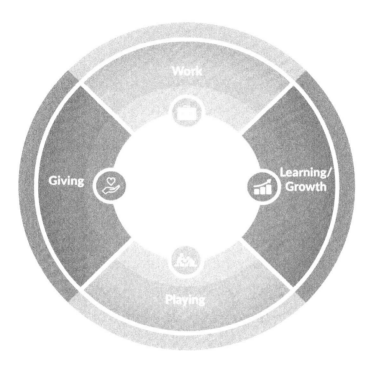

Figure 1

I use the above tool to set goals for myself. Starting in January of each year, I set two goals in each of the four segments of my life for the following two months. I write these goals out on a flip-chart size sheet of paper and pin the sheet of paper on the wall beside my desk. Over the two months I check in on these goals and see how I am progressing.

W: The **W**ork goals will relate to objectives connected to my coaching and training work

L: The **L**earning will relate to reading work-related books, relevant YouTube presentations, attending a workshop, peer-coaching, or a coaching supervision session; anything that I feel is relevant to my continuous professional development (CPD).

G: Giving could relate to doing some voluntary work, giving time to a friend or family member, making a donation – again anything that I consider relevant and appropriate to my definition of giving.

P: Playing is about setting aside time for my pastimes, hobbies, and the doing things that bring fun and enjoyment. Perhaps working on my game of golf, organising a social event with friends or family, a weekend away, a long luxurious bath, again whatever fits in with my definition of fun and recreation.

When working with a coachee it is important that I, as the coach, ask the coachee what the word Fun means to them? What does the word Giving mean to them? My idea and definition of Fun or Giving or any other word will be different to the coachee's definition. I have introduced this tool to many of my clients. and I have found it universally popular because of its simplicity and its achievability.

Case Study:

Paul is a member of the Executive Board of an organisation. During our session we explored different challenges he has at work. He recognised that as a result of the pressure of work he was not giving enough quality time to his family. When we discussed the Giving segment of the WLPG Wheel, he decided that he would set himself a goal of visiting his elderly mother at the weekend and bring his children with him. This would give his wife some downtime on her own, give him an opportunity to spend time with his mother, and strengthen his children's relationship with their granny.

Similarly, the coaching wheel may be broken into six or eight segments and the coach and coachee can use a template similar to the one below to co-design a wheel based on different topics that the coachee wants to explore.

Sample Wheel with Eight Segments
Figure 2

The coach asks the coachee open questions relating to each segment. The outcome of this discussion forms the basis for setting goals for future coaching sessions.

At the end of the coaching session, the coach may introduce the coachee to the twenty-one-day goal planning exercise (See Appendix 2).

See Appendix 3 for suggested questions in relation to the eight-segment wheel.

If a 'Wheel' is not used, the first session should cover a range of topics to assist the coachee in identifying priorities for the coaching session.

Executive Coaching Wheel

Similar to the Coaching Wheel, the Executive Coaching Wheel can form the basis of an exploratory conversation between the coach and coachee. The diagram below suggests different topics that the coachee may want to discuss. However, it is up to the coachee to change, substitute, or amend these suggested topics according to their needs. Through the conversation and the use of questioning techniques, the coach helps the coachee to explore what is working well at the moment, what they need to change, and what are the blocks and barriers to making those changes. Following on from this conversation, the coachee can begin to focus on what they want to achieve and goals they want to set for subsequent coaching sessions. When goals have been established, the coach and coachee can collaboratively design strategies for achieving the desired goals.

Case Study

Hugh is a senior executive in a large logistics organisation. He values his downtime and work/life balance is important to him. When we met for our first session, we co-designed a wheel that included segments from both the coaching wheel and the executive coaching wheel. He selected to work on the following segments from the coaching wheel: Physical surroundings (as he was renovating his home), Personal Development, and Fitness/Fun, and from the executive wheel selected to work on Time Management, Developing Strategy, Motivating Others, Budgeting, and Developing Relationships.

Other suggested topics for starting a coaching session are:

Tolerations

Ask the coachee what they are putting up with and they'll give you a list of between 5 and 500 things. On this list will be many important issues to focus the client on handling.

Shoulds

Find out what the coachee thinks they 'should' be doing right now, personally and professionally. It will indicate how much of someone else's life they are living.

Frustrations

What is frustrating the coachee? Ask, 'What are the five things that are frustrating you most right now' about,

- Themselves
- Their life
- Their work
- Other?

Desires

Examine unfulfilled desires. Find out what the client *really* wants in their personal/business life? What is the goal that they've given up on, or have put off for a while, due to circumstances?

Outcomes

Many coachees know exactly what they want and they want the coaches support to achieve it, so by all means help them reach these outcomes. Find out what they are.

Strategies

Some coachees want the coach to help them develop a strategy or a plan so they can achieve the result in the shortest period of time, with the least stress. If the coachee asks you 'how' they can achieve X, then you know they are asking for a strategy.

A change or improvement

Most coachees want to change or improve something. They may want to change jobs or improve a relationship. The trick is to discover if their 'change goal' is what they really want or if it is something they want to do because it will get them something else, as in, 'If I get a promotion, I'll be more fulfilled'.

(Source unknown).

How to structure a coaching session

The coaching session

Chemistry Call:

The first coaching session may be preceded by an initial call or face-to-face meeting. This step in the process is often called a Chemistry Call/Session and will typically last 20 to 30 minutes. The purpose of this call is to establish rapport and to check that both the coach and coachee are comfortable with each other and willing to work together in a formal coaching relationship.

During this session, the coach will ensure that the coachee understands how coaching differs from other interventions such as mentoring, consultancy, and counselling/therapy.

During this call/session, the coach should, in addition to building rapport, explain clearly a definition of coaching, cover the terms and conditions of the coaching contract, clarify any questions around confidentiality and explain that the collaborative coaching process is a non-advisory intervention, therefore the role of the coach is to empower the coachee to form actions and key takeaways from the session.

The logistics of the coaching session, such as the duration of each session, number of sessions, venue, cancellation policy, and fees should be agreed during the Chemistry session or before the first subsequent session commences. In the context of life coaching, such details may be confirmed in an informal e-mail. In executive or business coaching there may be a more formal written agreement. The content of the coaching agreement is described in further detail in chapter 1 in the section 'Collaborative Coaching Competencies'.

Step 1 – Coaching Topic

Following on from a successful Chemistry session, the terms and conditions of the coaching agreements will be agreed. A first coaching session is scheduled. At the start of the first session, the coach takes time to build the relationship, and establish rapport and trust. The coach will explain Confidentiality, Permission, and Responsibility (CPR as described in chapter 1, point 3 of Coaching Competencies). The coach clarifies what the coachee would like to work on during the session. The coachee may have a specific topic they wish to address or the coach may use a tool such as The Wheel of Coaching referred to earlier in the book to explore potential topics and desired goals with the coachee.

Step 2 – Use a coaching model such as the ARCH (Achieve, Relevant, Choices, Headway) model to work with the client. What is the reason for this?

In collaborative coaching the coach 'runs the coaching process' and ensures that there is a structure to the coaching session; a model such as the ARCH model provides the coach with a tried and tested framework. The coachee 'runs the agenda', that is, decides on the content of the coaching session. A coaching model such as the ARCH model is typically applied to each session and ensures that each coaching session follows a consistent process. It is not unusual for a coachee to have completed agreed actions/goals between sessions and to have a new goal or desired outcome at the start of subsequent sessions.

The ARCH coaching model (Achieve, Relevant, Choices, Headway)

A Simple Coaching Model

The ARCH model is a simple and effective model that can be applied to all coaching interactions. It is a model that is easily understood, easy to remember, and does not require specialist training to use. It can be applied to goal setting situations in both work and personal life and assumes that coachees are capable of making decisions, taking action, and committing to change. It is a behavioural model in that it develops behaviours through goal setting.

Effective coaches have the ARCH model or similar models internalised so that it becomes an unconscious competence (Fleishman, Dunnette, Howell & Alluisi, 1982).

It is important to understand that while any coaching model may appear to be a linear process, most coaching sessions are fluid and cyclical in nature. Therefore, it is important that the coach learns to use a coaching model with unconscious competence. It is like learning to ride a bike or to drive a car; with practice and training, the coach uses the model similar to when driving on auto-pilot. The model becomes so intrinsic to the coach that they do not have to think about each step in the model. The coach moves seamlessly back and forward between each step of the model. The model becomes the framework on which to structure the coaching conversation. A skilled coach has embedded the process so that it runs like a seamless coaching structure throughout the coaching session.

In a collaborative coaching session, the coach uses a combination of a coaching model such as the ARCH model and the SMART model to co-design meaningful outcomes with the coachee.

What do you aim to Achieve from the session? (A of the ARCH model)

Co-design and set clear, defined aims, goals and objectives with the coachee

Ask the coachee 'What do you wish to Achieve out of this coaching session/relationship?' What would a successful outcome look like to you?

Explore what the purpose is of achieving this goal.

Ask on a scale of 1 to 10 how important is achieving this goal to the coachee. If on a scale of 1 to 10 the coachee says it is a 4, explore with the coachee how committed they are to achieving this goal. Although the coachee may aim to achieve a particular outcome or goal, during the session this outcome may change or shift. This is okay as it is part of the exploration process. However, having a committed focus at the outset, sets the foundation for a meaningful conversation.

Demonstrate empathy and understanding, and show that you appreciate how important this goal is for the coachee. Be aware of and avoid bringing your own judgements, belief systems, and assumptions about this goal with you into the session.

Explore with the coachee:

- What are the benefits/costs/challenges to achieving this goal?

- How does this goal align with the coachee's value system? What other goals or aspirations conflict with this goal?

- What are the expectations of others?

- Who else (other stakeholders) needs to know about the goal?

- How will you inform them?

Goal and objective setting

What exactly is a goal or objective?

A goal or objective consists of a projected outcome which a person or a company plans or intends to achieve or bring about – it is a personal or organisational desired endpoint that is the result of an action plan and leads to some sort of change or development.

What is the reason for setting a goal?

- 'If there's no goal you can't score'

- Without a goal, there is no definition of success, which means wandering about hoping that success will find you

- Having goals allows for positive, directed action towards achieving success as defined by the goal

- When you set goals, you have clarity in what it is you want to achieve

- Having clarity allows focused action within a defined framework and lessens the likelihood of being diverted to other activities that don't further the achievement of the goal

- When there is a clear goal, you allow your subconscious mind into motion to begin working on achieving the goal

Working with people to allow them to clarify and set their goals is a very important part of the coaching process. Many people, however, have trouble setting goals, and even more people have problems achieving them.

Reflective Exercise

Write three goals that you want to achieve, check to see if they fulfil the above criteria.

Truly successful goals:

- Incorporate inspiring, motivating visions that overcome obstacles

- Involve thinking that is outcome-based rather than problem-rooted

- Are stated in positive language and avoid the language of defeat

- Are congruent with the central purpose of your life and are in line with your values

- Arise from asking ourselves life's most fundamental questions – underlying our goals is the search for meaning

Our deepest subconscious need is the search for meaning in our lives. To be truly happy, we need a sense of direction, and a sense of purpose. Happiness could be defined as the fullest realisation of worthy ideals. There is nothing more important to achieving success in life than clear knowledge of your true purpose in life. Happiness, success, and abundance flow from that certainty.

Coaching questions for setting goals:

Ask some essential questions.

- What do you *truly* want to achieve?
- What do you want from life?
- How clearly have you stated your goals?
- What does success look like for you?

Invite the coachee to write these goals down.

Case Study:

Sample conversation setting the scene and establishing the goal

The coach has completed a chemistry session with the coachee and they have agreed to work together for a number of sessions. Before starting into the coaching conversation, the coach took time to manage the contracting and introductions and establish rapport. The coach also clarified terms and conditions, and covered CPR (see chapter 1, point 3 in Coaching competencies) and set the scene by making sure pen, paper, and a glass of water was available to the coachee. The coach also ensured that the room had adequate lighting, was warm and ventilated, with appropriate seating.

Coach: 'What brings you here today? What goal or outcome would you like to achieve from our time together today?'

Coachee: 'Following on from our chemistry call the other day, there is one issue at work to which I want to find a solution. It is an HR issue. The issue relates to a key member of my team X, who is very competent in his work. He always achieves his work targets and, in truth, is a star performer. However, internally in the organisation he comes across as very arrogant and pushy. I have had several conversations with him and I am finding it hard to change him. After these conversations he changes for a short while but then reverts again after a while. This is having an impact on the team and on our relationship, but also is having an impact on his career and is doing him no favours. So in a nutshell that is where it is at, at the moment.'

Coach: 'So what I am hearing you say is that your goal from today's session is to look at options for how to manage X's negative behaviour in the workplace. This behaviour is impacting on X's relationship with his teammates and having an impact on his own career, and he is doing himself as well as the team a disservice.'

Reflective Exercise

What has happened so far? The coach started the conversation using open questions 'What brings you here today? What goal or outcome would you like to achieve from our time together today?'

The coachee has clearly identified a goal that he wants to work on. This process of exploring a potential outcome is fundamental to a successful collaborative conversation. I have found that it may take twenty or thirty minutes at the start of the conversation to get clarity on what is the desired outcome and on what a successful outcome looks like for the coachee. In my executive coach training courses, I use the analogy of climbing a mountain to explain this point. If you don't know what your goal is and where you want to go, be careful. You might end up climbing Mount Everest instead of Mount Kilimanjaro! The goal may change during the session – it may evolve or shift. However, it is fundamental to a successful session to collaborate and clarify what is the starting point for moving towards a successful outcome.

Relevant; scope out the current situation (R of the ARCH model)

Have the coachee self-assess, and give examples of what is relevant to the current situation at the moment.

- Let them tell their story. Invite self-assessment: what's happening, when does this happen, what effect does it have, other factors?
- What is the reality of the current situation?
- What are their fears and negative emotions that have stopped them from achieving this goal?
- Who do they know that has achieved that goal?
- What can they learn from them?
- When have they achieved something similar?

This exploration phase brings the coachee into a place of deep curiosity, openness and self-reflection. In the middle of challenging situations, the coachee may feel frustrated, judge themselves and others, doubt their own ability and narrow their vision of what is really happening. The purpose at this stage is for the coach to work with the coachee to understand objectively what is really happening and discover things exactly as they are. The coach can work with the coachee to see their own grievances and assumptions, question the validity of these and consider other people's perspectives. During this phase the coach works with the coachee to discover important and transformative insights and to discover things they didn't know that they didn't know.

Sample conversation continued:

The coachee has set a goal or outcome they want to achieve and given some relevant context for the situation. The next step is for the coach to clarify and gain agreement on the goal and continue to discuss and scope out the current situation. During this phase of the conversation, the coach will confirm with the coachee that they are on track and understand clearly what is not working and what are the challenges that need to be addressed.

Case Study, continued:

Coach: 'Okay, so it is good to hear what is relevant to the current situation. Just to clarify, X is a key member of the team and is quite target-driven. He is exceeding his targets. While this is one aspect of the relationship, he nevertheless shows inappropriate behaviours – I heard you use the word arrogance?'

Coachee: 'Yes, arrogance is a word I used. Sometimes he can come across as being arrogant to the point of being aggressive.'

Coach: 'Okay, so that is a behaviour you tried to tackle. Sometimes after addressing it, it changes but after a while he reverts to type and so causes friction and does himself a disservice. How accurate is that as a summary so far?'

Coachee: 'Yes, that is a fair observation of the position at the moment.'

Coach: 'So in terms of the current situation, what is the impact on colleagues?'

The coachee continues to describe the current situation, explaining that the impact on the team is that X disconnects from them. He behaves inappropriately during meetings, such behaviours include interrupting when others speak, texting, and continually checking his phone during meetings. The coachee explains that, on an individual basis, X can be rude and angry and bypass peers and colleagues with whom he should collaborate. Similarly, he bypasses the coachee (his manager) and goes to the coachee's Director when things are not 'going his way'. The coachee describes X's behaviour as one where he seeks to benefit himself to the detriment of his team and division.

The coach continues to ask open questions, to gather information, help the coachee to hear his story, clarify the current reality, and understand other peoples' perspective.

Coach: 'So how do you think he sees himself and his behaviour?'

Coachee 'I think that is at the core of the issue and is something I have had a conversation with him about before. I think his awareness of the situation is very low, despite feedback he has got from me and from others who he has worked with in previous roles. He has got feedback from his colleagues and also at a social level. He would be seen as being outside of the group, from the perspective of his peers and colleagues – people don't seem to warm to him. But from his self-awareness point of view, from discussions I have had with him, he is in the right; he is a perfectionist, and if he has to sacrifice the social element of it so be it – that is how he sees it. After these conversations he changes for a while and then reverts again.'

Coach: 'During those conversations, he seems to take some of the feedback on board for a few weeks. How has the feedback been received by him?'

Coachee: 'I think that is a very interesting question. The team is small and very closely knit – one that works well together, and they don't want disruption in the team, so when he does change his behaviour for the better, the team has commented on it to him and to me. It makes an instant improvement in the team dynamics.'

The coach then recaps briefly on the conversation to make sure they are hearing accurately what the coach is saying then proceeds.

Coach: 'So what are the instances where you see the behaviour reverting?'

Coachee: 'Hmmm. I think, my observation is that when he is conscious of his behaviour, he tries to control it, but normally it manifests itself when there is pressure, so when there is pressure on him, he tends to reflect it back to others on the team. Yes, so thinking about it, it is how he deals with pressure.'

The coach again clarifies back what she is hearing, reconfirms the original goal that X is a key member of the team, he has lots of good points and the coachee wants to support him. However, this arrogance is causing problems, and the coachee wants to explore options for managing X's adverse workplace behaviours.

Coach: 'Your experience of outcomes to date has been mixed, so what would you do differently now?'

Coachee: 'What I have done in the past is I have had one-to-ones with him and I have given him examples of his behaviours and the impact on team members. What I found is he has listened to what I have to say, but there is an element that he is in denial and that I am wrong and the team is wrong and I find that difficult to get over. So the reaction is to change his behaviour for a short while but there is no real long term change. I suppose the first thing is I have given him this feedback as part of his Performance Management review and we review that again during the year. The second thing is I don't wait for the annual and half-year review. If I notice instances of it during the course of the week or the month, I tend to call him aside and remind him of it, so I tend to do that and that is received quite well. He takes the feedback but again, I am not too sure he is convinced that he is the issue.'

Choices and possible solutions (C of ARCH model)

The coach explores potential choices and possibilities with the coachee by asking effective questions. Brainstorm options – as the coach, don't make suggestions but empower, ensure choice, ask open questions:

- What assumptions are you making that are blocking you from finding a solution?
- What are your thoughts and feelings in relation to this situation?
- How can you move towards the goal?
- What has worked in the past?
- What could you do as a first step?
- What else could you do?
- What would happen if you did nothing?
- What other choices and possibilities are there?
- What is a different way of doing this?
- What one thing could you do differently?

- Use the 'Yes ... and ...' questioning technique. The coachee comes up with an idea and the coach replies by saying 'Yes ... and what else is there or what else could you do?' It is a form of brainstorming where all suggestions are valid and appreciated and there is no judgement attributed to the suggestion.

During this phase of the conversation, the coach works with the coachee to find innovative and alternative solutions. A key element to the conversation is to facilitate the coachee to explore his limiting beliefs about how things should be, about looking at his behaviours and look for new and different ways of doing things. The coachee cannot control how other people behave or respond, he can only manage his own emotions and responses.

Case Study, continued

The coach moves further into facilitating the coachee to explore choices and possible solutions:

Coach: 'Okay, so what are the choices and possibilities that you can think of? Who are the key stakeholders you need to consider?

Coachee: 'So I suppose there are a couple of possible choices here. The first is about me learning to manage behavioural issues better and that is something I need to do better. I have managed a lot of people over the years. The good ones are always easy to manage. However, when there is difficulty, sometimes I think there is a development piece for me to learn like how to be a better manager of IR (industrial relations) type issues. The second thing is X's own development and behaviour. I think, in fact, in the same way that this coaching session has been of benefit to me, I think something similar for him would be a worthwhile investment, maybe even include a 360-degree emotional intelligence assessment so he can see his peers and direct reports' feedback in a formal report. I think it would be worthwhile. I want to avoid a disciplinary process if at all possible. However, it is an option if all else fails. At the end of it, I have to be seen to deal with this and I cannot allow my team to be negatively impacted by one person's behaviour, because it does impact.'

Coach: 'I am just curious. Can we go back to one thing you said there, that maybe we could explore a little more? What has stopped you or what feelings are conjured up in you when you are dealing with poor performance?'

Coachee: 'Oh, I am going to reflect on that for a moment.' (Silence for a short while, coach quietly sits and allows coachee to reflect and think). 'I think being only human and as humans, we like to give good news and we like to avoid conflict and to be liked.'

Coachee pauses again, coach sits in silence and waits.

Coachee: 'I think that is at the heart of it. I think I do okay and quite well, I... I... I speak to other managers in terms of ... Actually, that is something I might give as another option – to speak to other managers, who have had experience of similar situations. That is certainly another option. Coming back to the question you asked, I think I avoid conflict, and that is being very honest with you.'

Coach: 'And realising that you avoid conflict is okay. That is what today is about and sometimes acknowledging that can feel uncomfortable, and that is okay too. Sometimes it is about challenging ourselves and what we are bringing to the dynamic. And tell me, how have you managed similar situations in the past?'

Coachee: 'That is an interesting question. I remember one particular situation where I had to have a difficult conversation with a direct report. She was continually late and not meeting targets. It was a learning curve for me. I tried the softly, softly approach, offered constructive feedback about what she was doing well and got tears and excuses and all sorts of personal information. We discussed her seeking support through our employee assistance programme, however there was no change or shift in behaviour. In the end I had to tell her that the role was not working out and asked her what she was going to do about it. This took quite a while and many meetings where I simply had to keep reiterating my message that it was not working. In the end she decided to leave and go travelling. It was a slow process. To be honest it felt like death by a thousand daggers.

The difference was she wasn't meeting targets and was a poor performer and lacked any sort of commitment.'

Coach: 'Okay, so we have looked at different choices and possibilities and explored what has worked in the past. So looking at the current situation and how you are feeling and how the interactions are going, what steps are you going to commit to today?'

Coachee: 'Well I think the first thing is, having had the session here today … what it has done has brought clarity to a problem of mine. This problem has been niggling away for some time. It is something that I have pushed out. It is having a negative impact on the team and on myself and possibly on X, so I think what I will do first is acknowledge it as a key priority. The second thing, as I mentioned a couple of moments ago, is to have a conversation with a couple of other managers who I know might have had similar situations in the past, so I know that is something I can do. And a third option in terms of my own development is that I know that there are courses available that I could go on in relation to people and performance management.

Coach: 'Okay, so to clarify again, you discussed a number of choices and possibilities. One is to organise coaching for X and include a 360-degree assessment. How beneficial do you think that would be and how open do you think he would be with the idea?'

Coachee: 'I think it depends on how it is presented. I think if it presented as a punishment, it would be negatively received. I think if it is presented as a support and something positive for his career development it would be well received. I think on that basis it is a viable option, provided that we find the right coach to work with him.'

Coach: 'And then the other discussion point is in regards to your own development and finding the right course. How realistic is that in the context of being very busy? How achievable is it?'

Coachee: 'Yes, it is realistic. As I mentioned before, a big part of my role is managing a team and managing people. I have experienced some challenges in the past in managing challenging behaviours and I am sure in the future I will again. I think it is something I need to invest in and I will regard it as time well spent and be of benefit to me in the future.'

Coach: 'And the final thing we discussed is linking in with other managers who might have had similar experiences?'

Coachee: 'Yes.'

Coach: 'What other supports are available to you?'

Coachee: 'I can certainly have even an informal conversation with managers who have had similar experiences, and I could also connect with a colleague in HR and have an informal chat with her also. That would be a useful option as well.'

Coach: 'Okay, so you have a lot of choices open to you. So, from our discussions what do you want to focus on and move forward with?'

Coachee: 'Well I think I need to combine the three things we discussed, the coaching for X and for me to go on a course and deal with poor performers, and also have an off-the-record chat with some of my colleagues.'

How to make Headway? (H of ARCH model)

Wrap up by agreeing tactics and an action plan to achieve the goal. Agree on a time frame and gain commitment from the coachee. Identify specific steps and any obstacles, write an action plan. Continue to ask open questions:

- Where does this goal fit in with your priorities at the moment?
- What obstacles do you expect to meet? How will you overcome them?
- On a scale of one to ten, how committed are you to making headway and achieving this goal?
- What steps do you need to take to achieve this?

The purpose of this stage of the model is to move the coachee to action and to check in with the coachee about their commitment to achieving the goal. During this phase of the conversation, the coach can also use the SMART model as a form of checklist to assess the validity of the goal. At the end of the session, the coach also seeks feedback from the coachee about the session. How effective was the session for the coachee? The topic of seeking and giving feedback is discussed further later in this chapter.

SMART the Goal

Good goals are SMART goals.

- **S**pecific
- **M**easurable
- **A**ttainable
- **R**ealistic
- **T**angible/Time Frame/Trackable

Specific

Ensure the goal is specific. Clarify detail and avoid generalisation or lack of definition. Specific goals have a far greater chance of being accomplished than a general, wishy-washy goal. To set a specific goal consider the following 'W' questions:

Who: Who is involved?

What: What do I want to accomplish?

Where: Identify a location.

When: Establish a time frame.

Which: Identify requirements and constraints.

What the reason is: Specific reasons, purpose, or benefits of accomplishing the goal.

Measurable

Check that the goal is clearly measurable and progress is quantifiable

You need to establish concrete criteria for measuring progress so that you will know at any point where you are on your path to achieving your goal, and indeed, when you have achieved it. Ask the questions:

How much? How many?

Attainable

Confirm that the goal is attainable and appealing in the eyes of the coachee. For a goal to be attainable, the coachee should feel truly connected to the goal and want to achieve it. The best goals are those that are most important to the coachee, so determine how important the goal is. True goals grow naturally out of the purpose and passion in one's life.

When a coachee identifies the goals that are most important, they begin to figure out ways to make them come true. Check on a scale of one to ten whether the coachee is both willing and able to work towards the goal.

Realistic (does the coachee have the resources to carry out the goal?)

How realistic is the goal in terms of the coachee's existing life situation, and how relevant and ecologically good for all concerned? What support and conditions are important for the coachee to achieve the goal?

The first criterion is that the coachee must be willing and able to undertake the work towards achievement of the goal. No goal is realistically achievable if the coachee is not prepared to do the work to achieve it. Goals don't have to be set low to be achievable. Sometimes, high goals make us more motivated and therefore are more 'easily' achieved. It's also important to establish whether or not the coachee believes the goal is achievable.

Timebound

Ensure that the goal is timed, tangible, and trackable, having a schedule and ongoing evidence of progress.

If there's no timeframe, there's no sense of urgency and the goal will simply drift until it falls back into the 'wish' category. Attaching a timeframe to a goal gets one's subconscious mind into motion to begin working on achieving the goal. Having a timeframe also means the coachee can keep track of where he/she is on the path to achieving the goal. The coach should also check that the goal is tangible and that the coachee can almost experience it with all his/her senses: touch, taste, smell, sight, and hearing.

Case Study, continued

Coach: 'Okay, so we are going to SMART these options. What I mean by that is that we are going to check in to see that each goal is Specific, Measurable, Achievable, Realistic, and Timebound. In the context of getting a coach for X, how specific is the goal to get the support for X? In the context of finding the right course for yourself, how specific is that as a goal for yourself? And in the context of the off-the-record conversations, how specific is that as a goal to work on also?'

Coachee: 'Yes, I am going to have a chat with X about the benefits of coaching and doing a 360-degree assessment, speak to HR about a relevant course and have a chat with some of my colleagues about their experiences of similar situations.'

Coach: 'So what would be the measure, what would success look like?'

Coachee: 'For me the measure would be seeing a long term and sustained shift in X's behaviour and also in my comfort with having difficult conversations and dealing with poor performers.'

Coach: 'And how achievable is that?'

Coachee: 'Yes. It is achievable. I would consider it time well spent to focus on this. So I will give priority to it.'

Coach: 'How realistic is this as a goal? What might be the obstacles?'

Coachee: 'It is quite realistic. To be honest, I have been a bit lazy and hesitant about doing this, but now that I have talked about it, it is very relevant and realistic. I can't see any reason not to do it.'

Coach: 'That is good to see the shift in mindset from something that was "over there" to "over here". So, what about a timescale; when would you see yourself doing this?

Coachee: 'I work in Head Office so I can check in with HR immediately, there is nothing holding me back on this.'

Coach: 'So to wrap up and summarise, when you came in you talked about this key individual, the impact he was having on you, on the team and your concerns about his future as a result of his behaviour. He is a good employee and achieves his targets, however, his behaviour is an issue. So we explored the situation and then moved on to look at some options. The first was coaching and to develop him. The second was to speak to other managers and hear their stories. The third was to look at your own management style, specifically around managing poor performance. We discussed and agreed outcomes for two of the options and you made a commitment to taking action in relation to both of the actions.'

Coachee: 'Yes, that is all a very fair summary.'

Coach: 'Okay, so having worked through this, how does it feel?'

Coachee: 'Well, as a result of the session, I am confident that I have come away with an action plan that will be of benefit to both myself, the team, and X.'

Coach: 'So on a scale of one to ten how committed do you feel?'

Coachee: 'I am going to give myself a commitment of ten on this. It has bugged me for a while and it has given me a very clear vision of what my options are. I am in a very positive place in terms of resolving this.'

Coach: 'So as a wrap-up, how did the session work for you today and when would it suit you to schedule our next session?'

Coachee: 'I am very pleasantly surprised at how being able to reflect in a structured way has been very helpful, and I look forward to putting those options into practice, so thank you. It would be good to meet again in three weeks and follow up on progress.'

SMART – Other Models

While the best known and most widely used is the SMART model, there are other models in circulation. For example, some say goals should 'Smarten Up'

- Enthusiastic

Client should be motivated to take the journey

- Natural

Working out of natural instincts and congruent attitudes

- Understood

By partners, teammates and 'significant others'

- Prepared

For some possible setbacks or misunderstandings

Others say create IMPRESS-ive goals:

- Individual

Reliant on your actions

- Measurable

Able to gauge progress

- Positive

Frame 'for', never 'against'

- Realistic

Push out the boundaries, know how far and believe in yourself!

- Ecological

Good for you and the world

- Specific

Clear and without ambiguity

- Sustainable

Have they a future?

Select the model that best fits you and best fits your client.

Reflective Exercise

Review the three goals from the previous exercise. Re-write them as SMART, SMARTEN Up or IMPRESS-ive goals.

Asking for feedback

For many coaches, this can seem a rather daunting process. Typically, a coach will seek feedback at the end of each coaching session. The purpose of the coach seeking feedback is for the coachee to have the opportunity to reflect on what has worked well during the session and what if anything they would like to explore further at subsequent sessions. It also provides the opportunity for the coachee to discuss if they are unhappy about anything in the coaching relationship or about the coaching process. Simple open questions such as 'What worked well during the session?', 'What would you like to do more of?' or 'What you would like to do less of in future sessions?' opens the door for feedback about the process rather than the coach.

Giving feedback to the coachee

Sometimes as a coach it is important to give feedback either during or at the end of the session. Essentially, feedback is a mechanism to enable human beings to develop and improve and change. One myth we often encounter is that feedback is always negative, that it is always a description of a person's inadequacies and failures. However, it is important to feed back successes. Positive feedback is as important as negative feedback.

Research shows that for a person to be emotionally at their best, they need the following ratios between positive feedback/messages and negative feedback/messages:

> Worldwide average 5:1 positive feedback/messages to negative feedback/messages
>
> Irish average 7:1 positive feedback/messages to negative feedback/messages
>
> Team average 3:1 positive feedback/messages to negative feedback/messages

Research by Barbara Fredrickson, Maureen Gaffney and John Gottman (Gaffney, 2016)

Feedback is one of the most important aspects of self-development. Feedback enables us to find out how other people see us and to know whether their perception of us agrees with our own. An enhanced level of self-awareness will help us to grow and develop. A coachee can increase their self-awareness in two ways:

- By listening to themselves in order to have a better understanding of their feelings and reactions to the ways they approach events in life.
- By requesting feedback from others on how they see and react to you. During the coaching session the coach can feed back to the coachee their intuitions, insights, and reflections.

When facilitating coaching training and communications courses, I break participants into groups of three (triads). One participant brings a goal to the session, one participant plays the role of coach and uses the ARCH model and the third participant observes and gives feedback to the coach on their coaching skills. The observer learns and enhances their coaching skills from observing the ebb and flow of the coaching sessions and also learns the skill of delivering effective feedback to the coach. The coach gets objective feedback into what worked well and what could be improved upon. Each person in the triad then swaps roles so that they all have the opportunity to role-play being the coach, coachee, and observer.

Reflective Exercise

List as many barriers as you can to soliciting feedback.

Potential barriers to soliciting feedback from others:

- Fear that they will focus only on weaknesses
- They may tell me things I did not know about
- I might get information I am not ready for
- I might feel hurt by what is said
- I am uncomfortable with compliments
- I might be seen as 'fishing for compliments'
- The other person might be embarrassed at being asked
- The request for feedback might be seen as insecurity or weakness
- I am not sure I will get the truth

Consider the following strategies for overcoming these barriers:

Barriers to Soliciting Feedback	Ways of Overcoming Them
• Fears about getting painful negative information.	• Start by asking specific questions about safe areas • Ask for some positive and some negative feedback • Only ask for feedback from people you know genuinely value you • Give yourself time to talk through any hurt you might feel, but don't blame the other person

• Fears about other person's reaction:
  o Not sure how the other person will react
  o Might embarrass the other person
  o Not sure that I will get the truth
	• Choose someone with whom you have a formal relationship where feedback can be seen as a normal part of that relationship, e.g. your boss, a regular client, a subordinate
	• Choose a close friend
	• Contract with a colleague to give each other honest positive and negative feedback on a regular basis

• Unable to deal with positive feedback and compliments.	• Practice by acknowledging to yourself when you've done something well • Write down a list of all the things you're good at • Write down a list of things you like about yourself

Ongoing sessions

The contract may include a specific number of sessions or may progress on a session-by-session basis.

For each subsequent session

Review the coachee's mood and current situation – this means checking how the person feels, what has happened and where they believe they are now. Check on the assignment progress since the last session – what does the person believe they have learned? What went well? What could have been done differently? Very often a coachee will have dealt with the preceding goal and will have other outcomes that they want to discuss as subsequent sessions. However, this should not become a focus of the session.

Once I have reviewed the progress from the previous session, I will then explain to the coachee that this is their time and space and check with them what they would like to explore or work on in this session.

When using coaching as a manager rather than in an executive coaching role, the focus of follow-up sessions may be more operational and focused on task fulfilment.

Make an issue list

Make an 'issue list' for the current or initial session – the coachee may choose something from the original and ongoing agenda, or want to develop something they have discovered from undertaking the assignment.

Reviews

Although each session has a space through the feedback mechanism for a mini review session at the end, it can be helpful to set specific dates for more formalised reviews. For example, if there is an agreed six-session programme, you might set a formal review after every second session.

Review questions

The coach can ask the coachee at the previous session to consider three questions for discussion at the review as follows:

- Where were you when you first started the coaching process?
- Where are you now?
- What else do you feel you need to do?

Reviews should work both ways – the review also provides an opportunity for the coachee to provide their feedback.

Self-Coaching: using a coaching model on yourself

To improve your performance and develop a roadmap to your personal success, you can also use coaching models on yourself: identify specific goals you wish to achieve; assess the current situation; list your options and make choices; and, finally, make steps towards your goal specific, and define timing.

Chapter 5: Communications and Building Rapport

'The single biggest problem in communication is the illusion that it has taken place' – *George Bernard Shaw*

In this chapter you will:

- Define and examine how communications are transmitted
- Learn about the components of communication: words, body language, tone, and pitch of voice
- Learn about Mirror, Matching, Leading, and Pacing
- Listening skills – the three levels of listening
- Active listening techniques
- Communications in a digital age

Definitions:

Communications

First, the word communicate is a verb. It is something we do, an activity that we undertake to:

- Convey information: *Oxford English Dictionary*
- Transmit information, thoughts or feelings: *Wordnet*

Communication, on the other hand, is a noun. It is:

> 'A process by which information is exchanged between individuals through a common system of symbols, signs or behaviour' – *Merriam-Webster Dictionary*

The sustained ability to develop relationships is a cornerstone of successful communications. Effective communications can be achieved through techniques such as listening with a non-judgemental, authentic, and respectful understanding. This may include listening to the other person's perspective, even though their perspective may not be in keeping with your own personal belief system, values, or mindset.

In our day-to-day communications, we often forget that communication is about a receiver and a sender. The sender assumes the receiver understands the message and places the burden of accountability on the receiver. The receiver omits to check back for understanding and clarification and each party to the conversation fails to recognise that there is another person on the other side of the human equation. The ability to ask simple, powerful, and open questions is a core communication skill. Through the act of asking powerful questions, we seek to gain understanding and develop mutually beneficial collaborative relationships. This is what we call engagement and the art of building rapport.

However, building rapport comprises more than sending and receiving verbal messages. Building rapport is made up of multiple skills such as understanding the context, congruence and clusters of body language signals and tonality of voice, as well as the actual words spoken. If I am standing at a bus stop on a cold day and not wearing a coat, and I have my arms and legs crossed and my teeth are chattering, the context and the cluster of body language signals does not suggest that I am being defensive. It suggests that I am cold. If, however, given the same body language signals, I am standing in front of my boss and being spoken to, once again, about lateness to work, this same context and cluster of body language signals suggest that I am uncomfortable about receiving feedback and possibly defensive. Understanding the role of micro facial expressions and other subliminal messages that we pick up from each other further enhances our ability to develop the skill of communications.

Reflective Exercise

Consider what appeals to you from a communications perspective.

Attributes list 1:

Warm	Honest
Friendly	Exciting
Interested	Knowledgeable
Organised	Creative
Confident	Inspiring
Open	Authentic
Informal	Funny

What is the reason the above attributes appeal/or do not appeal?

Attributes list 2:

Pompous	Vague
Flat	Complex
Patronising	Nervous
Formal	Irrelevant
Stuffy	Monotonous
Intense	Closed

What is the reason the above attributes appeal/or do not appeal?

How do we communicate?

- Words
- Voice
- Body Language/Non-Verbal Communications

To create an understanding of the message and establish rapport, the impact of three above-mentioned areas need to match the message

Listening – Listening to tone and being aware of the coachee's body language is also crucial to successful collaborative coaching and establishing rapport.

Communications we deliver are composed of:

Words	7%
Voice	38%
Body Language	55%

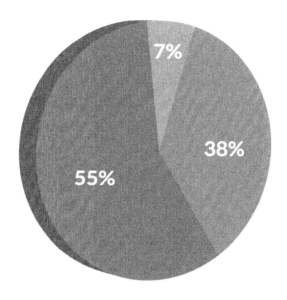

Mehrabian, A. and Ferris, L., *'Inference of attitudes from nonverbal communication in two channels'*, The Journal of Counselling Psychology, Vol 31, 1967.

Words

Generally, we access information through our senses: we see (visual), hear (auditory), and feel (kinaesthetic). To process and store this information, we make pictures in our minds of what we believe we have seen, sounds of what we believe we have heard, sensations of what we believe we have felt. Some of us assimilate information through facts, figures, and logic (auditory digital).

Type of words based on the senses

- See (visual)
- Hear (auditory)
- Feel (kinaesthetic)
- Taste (gustatory)
- Smell (olfactory)
- Auditory digital (logic)

Often people have a preferred 'system'. For example, when learning something new, some of us may prefer to see it or imagine it performed (visual), others like to hear how to do it (auditory), others choose to get a feeling for it (kinaesthetic), and yet others make sense of it (auditory digital).

People from the Western world tend to access information predominantly through visual, auditory, kinaesthetic, and auditory digital channels. Those from the Eastern hemisphere frequently use gustatory (taste) and olfactory (smell) to take in information from their surroundings.

In the book 'Midnight's Children' by Salman Rushdie (Rushdie, 2013), an Indian author, he uses descriptions such as

- 'Things, even people, have a way of leaking into each other like flavours when you cook'
- 'His sense of smell is so intense he can smell any or all odours no matter how small, he can smell emotions, fear, happiness'
- 'Smell and taste of the chutneys, spices and pickles'

Research conducted by Master Training Inst. suggests the following breakdown for people:

- Auditory – 7% showed a preference for receiving information across this channel
- Visual – 51% showed a preference for receiving information across this channel
- Kinaesthetic – 42% showed a preference for receiving information across this channel

The same research indicated what people remembered twenty-four hours after receiving different pieces of information across the three channels:

- Auditory information recalled correctly – 38%
- Visual information recalled correctly – 81%

- Kinaesthetic information recalled correctly – 77%

With the exception of the kinaesthetic sense, all the other sensory organs are located close to the brain, which is the main information processor in our human body. The main kinaesthetic sensory organ – the hands – take in information through experiential means such as touching and feeling. The number of nerve connections between the brain and hands is greater than between any other organ in the body. Hands have over 25% of the total nerve connections to the brain.

As a coach, it might be helpful to be aware of our own preferred system and to be aware of our clients' preferred systems and develop the ability to use all of these systems to communicate effectively with our clients, choosing the one most appropriate for the situation.

A person's preferred system can be deduced from the words that they use. For example:

Visual:

- I see what you mean
- The solution looks bright
- Can I see some more detail?

Auditory:

- He's calling the tune

- Loud and clear
- Can I hear some more detail?

Kinaesthetic:

- I've got a handle on that
- I can't put my finger on it
- Can I get a feel for more detail?

Auditory digital

- That's logical
- I'll take it under advisement
- Can you provide me with more detail?

As a coach, listen for clues as to the type of modality a coachee uses through the types of words they use. I work with many executives who work in the engineering and finance sectors. The type of words they use tend to be auditory digital. One person I worked with was a qualified civil engineer working in a manufacturing company. I was aware that when talking to her it was important to use auditory digital type words. So rather than phrase a question 'How do you feel about this issue?' I would ask the question 'What do you think about this issue?'

Words – past, present, future

Where in time do you put your attention?

- Some people live their lives in the past
- Some people live in the moment, their attention is on the present
- Some people are continually planning and living in the future

As a coach, listen for clues as to the time-space occupied by a coachee.

Reflective Exercise

What clues can you look for during a conversation?

Voice

Tone of voice is about your ability to convey meaning through how you say something rather than what you say. When delivering coach training and communications courses, one of the exercises I include goes as follows: I say 'good morning' five times and each time I use a different tonality and pitch of voice. I ask the participants to identify which of the following expressions, Anger, Sarcasm, Vulnerability, Delight, and Indifference, I am conveying each time I say 'good morning'.

Reflective Exercise

What level of awareness do you have about tonality and pitch of voice when listening to others speak?

I know for myself, auditory skills are not a key strength of mine. I struggle to pick up on tonality. I can hear the quiver in a person's voice if nervous because of their breathing, however, other than that, I often have to clarify with a coachee about the meaning of a statement if an emotion or expression is expressed through tonality rather than the words used.

Body Language

Body language, gestures such as eye-contact, showing passion, nodding, being relaxed and smiling plays a vital role in creating a positive rapport with the client.

How do we convey information in a nonverbal manner?

Constituting up to 55% of what we are communicating, body language is a vital part of communications as a coach. If you wish to communicate well, then it makes sense to understand how you can use your body language to work with a coachee. Body language is the gateway to a person's emotions.

According to Prof Brown and Brown in *Neuropsychology for Coaches* (Brown & Brown, 2012), there are eight basic emotions. The first four emotions listed are what we call survival emotions i.e. they are activated when we feel threatened. Surprise is the only emotion that we can experience simultaneously with other emotions e.g. we can experience fear and surprise simultaneously, we can experience happiness and surprise simultaneously. However, we cannot experience fear and happiness simultaneously. All consumer behaviour is based on accessing our emotions of happiness and love. The eight basic emotions are:

- Fear
- Anger
- Disgust
- Sadness
- Shame
- Surprise
- Happiness
- Love

What is the significance of body language constituting 55% of what we are communicating? Have you ever been in a situation where, although a person says something, you feel that the words lack authenticity or honesty? On the basis that body language constitutes 55% of our communications, it is likely that you are picking up on subliminal body language signals which appear to contradict what the person is saying.

Let's look at an example. A person is talking about the importance of inclusivity and equality, yet for some reason you are not convinced about the authenticity of the message. Observe the hand signals. Where a person is using palms facing down or closed hand gestures the person observing the hand gesture will interpret the message negatively. Is this what is happening when you interact with this person? Contrast this with a person using a palms facing up or open position when delivering a message.

According to research, this gesture is interpreted by the listener as a positive message. When the hand signals or other body language signals are not congruent with the message being delivered, we refer to this as 'body language leakage'. Body language gestures (55%) speak louder than the words (7%)! Similarly, Paul Ekman studied micro facial expressions and recognised that fleeting facial expressions may reveal a person's true emotions and contradict what a person is saying. A person may say they like the taste of the meal you are serving, however a fleeting wrinkling of the nose and pulling back of the lips may convey a different message.

Studies of nervous travellers at airports demonstrate what is known as displacement activities such as constant checking of passports, tickets and items in pockets such as wallets (the reassuring tap), and other constant fidgeting gestures.

I recall a coaching session where the coachee suddenly started to jiggle one of his feet up and down while telling me a story. I immediately noted this shift and change in body language behaviour. When he finished his story, I asked him what was really going on in that particular situation. It transpired there was another layer to the story that he had not revealed.

A word of caution. A coach needs to be aware that people make assumptions about body language gestures that are not accurate. A person standing at a bus stop with his/her arms and legs crossed (usually interpreted as closed body language) and teeth chattering as a result of a biting wind is not demonstrating that they are putting up a barrier between themselves and others. Clearly, they are protecting themselves from the uncomfortable weather conditions.

When interpreting body language gestures the coach should take into account the three C's of body language.

The three C's of body language are Context, Congruence, and Clusters.

In the above example, the context is standing at a cold, windy bus stop, the congruence is the consistency between the message the person is speaking and the body language, and the cluster of body language signals is the crossing of arms and legs and chattering teeth.

In contrast, a coachee that is sitting near to you and says that they are being open and honest and yet has arms and legs crossed and is not making good eye-contact does not demonstrate congruence between what they are saying and how they are behaving. Nor is the coachee demonstrating a context or situation that demonstrates openness. There is also a cluster of more than one body language signal (crossed legs and arms) that suggest a discrepancy between what is being said and what the body language suggests. Again, in any collaborative coaching session, checking in and clarifying with the coachee about the information being conveyed is fundamental to the success of the session. Although it is not a preferred way of coaching, in some instances coaching may take place on the phone. There, tone and pitch of voice, silence, pauses, and sighs can be informative about the coachee's mood and mindset.

Communications using Leading and Pacing

The best coaches are those who use rapport to enter the world of the coachee.

Rapport allows you to build a bridge to the other person. When rapport is established, it is possible that you can then begin to change your behaviour and the coachee is likely to follow. This is also called Leading and Pacing.

- Pacing

This involves matching someone for a while.

- Leading

This involves changing your behaviour and the person following. If this is achieved unconsciously, it suggests you have achieved rapport. From a business perspective, building successful relationships involves building trust and rapport. Trust and rapport comprise three elements:

- Competence

How knowledgeable are you about your field of expertise?

- Reliability

How conscientious and dependable are you?

- Ability to connect

How effective are you at connecting at an emotional level with others?

Reflective Exercise

How good is your ability to listen and seek to understand other people's perspectives, even if they go against your thoughts and beliefs?

Mirroring and matching

Rapport is established by:

- Mirroring

When you match a person's body language

When you unobtrusively synchronise your body language to match a person's posture and gestures, the person will feel comfortable with you and relaxed, and the development of rapport is facilitated. As a coach we want to encourage the development of rapport; it serves us well to adjust our postural and nonverbal signals to match those of our coachee. If they lean forward, you lean forward too. If that person relaxes and leans back in the chair, do the same. This synchronisation, however, must be subtle, so that the coachee is unaware of your mirroring activities and does not think that you are disingenuously copying their every move.

- Matching

When you match a person's language/words

You can also synchronise your language and words, and vocal tone and pace to match the other person's. If the person speaks softly and slowly, for instance, lower your volume and speak at a slower pace than your normal rate. Often, a slow talker can irritate a faster speaker. A quiet, soft-spoken individual may not feel as comfortable with a loud, boisterous speaker. A coach needs to be able to adjust their style to match that of their coachee. Again, this enhances the opportunity for rapport development.

In addition, you can use your words to connect with your coachee's preferred sensory system. With visual clients, for instance, speak about how things look, with auditory clients, discuss how things sound, for those who are kinaesthetic consider how things feel and for an auditory digital person ask them what they think, rather than feel, hear, or see.

Listening skills

> 'So when you are listening to somebody, completely, attentively, then you are listening, not only to the words, but also to the feeling of what is being conveyed, to the whole of it, not part of it.' – Jiddu Krishnamurti 1895–1986 Indian Theosophist

Fundamental to collaborative coaching is the skill of active listening. According to Whitworth, Kimsey-House, Kimsey-House and Sandahl in Co-Active Coaching, active listening combines rapport building skills with an authentic, sincere, and genuine curiosity and interest in others. Active listening is about picking up on signals and cues; it is about listening to what is being said but also about listening to what is not being said. It is about a 360-degree intuition where the listener is in sync with the other person, can stay connected, and find common ground. Active listening arises from authentic communications and a desire to connect at a human level, rather than at a transactional level where the objective is to maximise the outcome for yourself.

Listening is a talent that each of us is given in some measure. Collaborative coaches have developed the ability to listen at a very deep level. It is a skill that can be trained and developed. Collaborative coaches have taken the skill of listening and brought it to a high level of proficiency.

Reflective Exercise

We have two ears and only one mouth – what level of the talking-to-listening ratio should you use?

A collaborative coach listens at many levels at once to hear where the coachee is in their process. The coach is listening for the nuance of hesitation, for the ring of something not quite true, for belief systems and barriers to progress. Even in telephonic coaching, it is possible to hear much more than the words of the story.

There's a great deal of information conveyed in a conversation's tone and pacing that the coach hears, especially after getting to know the coachee.

Signs that you are not listening actively:

- You feel critical of a coachee's vocabulary, grammar, or accent

- You want to give advice and allow this to interfere with non-judgemental listening
- You tell the coachee about your experience

There are three levels of listening.

> Level 1 – Internal Listening
>
> Level 2 – Focused Listening
>
> Level 3 – Active or Global Listening

Level 1 – Internal Listening

At level 1 our focus is on ourselves.

We listen to the words of the other person but the focus is on what it means to us. At level 1 the spotlight is on me: my thoughts, my judgements, my feelings, my conclusions about myself and others. Whatever is happening with the other person is coming back to me through a one-way energy trap that lets selected information in.

At level 1 we ask ourselves the question – 'What does this mean to me?'

If your attention is on trying to figure out what to say next – what brilliant question to put to the client – that should be a clue that you are listening at level 1: inside your own experience.

Signs of listening at level 1, also known as passive listening

- Constantly judging what is being said against our values – assessing as good, bad, worthy, unworthy
- Once the listener makes a decision they stop listening, waiting for the other person to stop talking so they can say what they want
- Typical behaviours – questioning the facts, disagreeing, shaking the head to show disagreement
- May be relevant when you need to make a quick decision, but may limit your success in other communication situations
- Acting busy and distracted, focused on own goals
- Drifting into your own thoughts
- Losing focus easily
- Listening to a person while looking at another person in the room (known as MIPPERS i.e. looking at More ImPortant PERSons)

Level 2 – Focused Listening

At level 2 there is a sharp focus on the other person (e.g. people's posture – leaning towards each other). For a coach, all the listening at level 2 is directed at the client.

At level 2 your awareness is totally on the other person. You listen for their words, their expression, their emotion, everything they bring.

You notice what they say and how they say it. You notice what they don't say. You see how they smile or hear the emotion in their voice. You listen for what they value. You listen for their vision and what makes them energetic. You listen for what makes them come alive in the coaching session and what makes them go dead or withdraw.

At this level, the impact of listening is on the speaker. The coach is like a perfect mirror that absorbs none of the light; what comes from the client is returned.

Most coaching happens at least at level 2. It is the level of empathy, creativity, clarification, collaboration, and innovation.

Level 3 – active or global listening

At level 3, you listen and take in not just the words but also the meaning of what is being said. To achieve active listening, a coach can use techniques such as paraphrasing, reflecting, and summarising.

Paraphrasing

The aim of paraphrasing is to tell the client what you hear: Some possible introductory phrases for paraphrasing:

- So, what I hear you saying is...
- It sounds like you...
- If I understand you correctly...

- You are telling me that…

Example

- Client: 'I am completely worn out – it's twice as difficult for me to get around now with a physical disability, and my family think I am feeling sorry for myself.'

- Coach: 'So what I hear you saying is that you are exhausted trying to adjust to the situation and your family don't seem to be able to understand.'

Reflecting

The aim of a reflection is to help the client feel understood, accepted, and encouraged to share more of their feelings. It is about expressing empathy!

Example

- Client: 'I'm just wasting your time. There must be others who have much more serious problems than me.'

- Coach: 'You sound as if you are worried that your problems are not important enough.'

When I facilitate coaching training and communications courses and team coaching sessions, one exercise I use goes as follows:

I ask the participants to divide into groups. One person tells a story about a meaningful event, it does not have to be a deeply personal event but one that they remember because it was emotionally important to them. When giving the instructions for the exercise, I tell the listeners that when the storyteller is finished, they must tell the storyteller **what they heard.** The purpose of the exercise is that rather than the listener giving a detailed account of the story, the listener should explain to the storyteller what emotions they heard being expressed in the story. Reflecting back to a person means reflecting the emotional meaning of the story rather than the detail of what was said. This is a key skill of level 3 listening.

Summarising

The aim of summarising is to pull together the main strands/points of a discussion and organising the discussion so it can be reviewed, confirmed, or corrected (Moursund, 1990).

Example:

- Coach: 'May I just check that I have understood this correctly? You have told me of a few choices open to you. You could try ringing your sister-in-law directly and telling her how you feel, you could approach your brother, or you could give the situation more time to see what happens.'

One of the benefits of level 3 listening is greater access to your intuition. From your intuition, you receive information that is not directly observable, and you use that information just as you'd use words coming from the client's mouth. At level 3 listening, you take in information, demonstrate curiosity, question, respectfully challenge and then you notice the impact.

- How did your questions, insights, reflections land?
- What did you notice about the coachee?

The key to level 3 listening is simply to take the information, use it, and see what emerges. Everything in coaching hinges on listening – especially listening with the coachee's agenda in mind:

- How on track is the coachee with their vision?
- How are they honouring their values?
- Where are they today, and where do they want to go to?

When listening at level 3, the coach taps into their own intuition whilst understanding at a visceral level the coachee's triggers and responses.

Listening is the entry point for all coaching. When listening at level 3, the coach taps into an intuitive sense of the right next question, the path to be taking through the coaching session, to probe what is not being said by the coachee. The coach therefore can support the coachee to validate and encourage these unspoken words and thoughts.

Listening at level 3, then, is the gate through which all the coaching should pass. When a coach listens at level 3, it builds a foundation of non-judgemental, empathetic trust where the coachee feels validated, acknowledged, and more open to expressing vulnerability. This collaborative alliance opens the door for the coach to challenge and provoke the coachee to think and reflect in a supportive and creative environment and for the coachee to become more self-aware and gain a deeper insight into their motivations, biases, and judgements.

Silence:

The word LISTEN contains the same letters as the word SILENT. Being comfortable with silence and allowing the coachee time to process thoughts, feelings, and information is a critical coaching skill.

Reflective Exercise

How comfortable are you with allowing silence during a conversation?

Coaching Technique: Reframing – 'Every cloud has a silver lining'

To reframe means to consider the issue from many different aspects. As a coach we can work with a coachee to see the 'gift' in what appears to be a negative situation.

Reflective Exercise

Think about a time when you experienced the following situations. How could you reframe them to see a positive outcome from what was a seemingly negative experience?

- Failure
- Missed opportunity
- 'Mistakes'
- Financial loss
- Stress
- Difficult relationships
- Competitive threats

Three barriers to good listening

1. Preoccupation in the coach's mind with a personal issue.

Coaches are human too; it is important for a coach to self-manage their own energy level and emotional state. In the event a coach is going through a deep personal issue, the effect may be to render coaching less effective, and the coach should consider rescheduling the session until a time when they can be client-centred.

2. Listening to the language but not the tone and resonance in the client's voice can lead to misunderstanding and poor listening.

Even on the phone, the majority of the message is not held in the actual words spoken. It is delivered in the tone, pace, resonance, and silences between the words. The good listener uses their level 2 and especially level 3 listening skills to get inside the client's bubble and see the words from the client's perspective. This involves a high client focus, and the freedom gained by not directing the conversation helps here too.

3. Haste from the coach to 'run' the coaching process, or direct the conversation, will break the bond of trust and could lead the client to becoming less open.

The barriers can lead to missed opportunities to reveal the correct path for a client to achieve a set of goals.

Any listener is unlikely to find unsolicited advice beneficial. It may irritate, and such advice may suggest that the coach has not understood or listened deeply enough to the story. The coachee may feel that their thinking or story is faulty and therefore feel undermined. If the coach does not validate and listen to the coachee's story and try to see the world through the coachee's perspective, the coachee may become defensive. When a coachee feels listened to and understood, there is a greater likelihood of the coachee letting down his/her guard, relaxing, and beginning to open up and trust the relationship. It is at this stage that the opportunity for exploring options, challenging, and 'pushing-back' can become effective interventions.

Coaches use all their practical experience to remain focused on their client and their needs at all times during the session. This is the beauty and simplicity of good coaching. It's a friend with *no* personal agenda.

Listening – A philosophy

You are not listening to me when:

- You do not care about me.

- You say you understand before you know me well enough.
- You have an answer for my problem before I've finished telling you what my problem is.
- You cut me off before I've finished speaking. You finish my sentences for me.
- You feel critical of my vocabulary, grammar, or accent. You are dying to tell me something.
- You tell me about your experience, making mine seem unimportant. You are communicating to someone else in the room.
- You refuse thanks by saying you really haven't done anything.

You are listening to me when:

- You come quietly into my private world and let me be me.
- You really try to understand me even if I'm not making much sense. You grasp my point even when it's against your own sincere conviction. You realise that the hour I took from you has left you a bit tired and drained.
- You allow me the dignity of making my own decisions even though you think they might be wrong.
- You do not take my problem from me, but allow me to deal with it in my own way.

- You hold back your desire to give me good advice.
- You do not offer me religious solace when it is not appropriate.
- You give me enough room to discover for myself what is really going on. You accept my gift of gratitude by telling me how good it makes you feel to know that you have been helpful. – *Author unknown*

Communications and Coaching in a Digital Age

> 'Precision of communication is important, more important than ever, in our era of hair-trigger balances, when a false or misunderstood word may create as much disaster as a sudden thoughtless act.' *James Thurber 1894 – 1961*

Thurber's words, despite being written in the last century, reflect the potential pitfalls with coaching in the modern digital age. We are exposed to 24/7 information. Communications methods have multiplied and messaging has become instantaneous. Words matter, customs and culture matter. In the digital age where working and dealing with people has become borderless, incorrect use of language or not understanding cultural nuances may result in a breakdown in communications and disharmony. In today's digital world where full-time connectivity is now the norm, it is relational proximity rather than physical proximity that is of primary influence. For coaching to be effective, be it through digital or face-to-face means, it has to connect with people at a core level. Coaching can successfully take place using a digital medium such as a web-based video conferencing service. However, if at all possible, make the first meeting face-to-face. Virtual communications can be fraught with challenges, can take more time and need to be managed more closely. Building trust and rapport is as important in virtual coaching as in face-to-face coaching, so too is constantly clarifying and checking back for understanding. Be aware that in a digital world, the value of human connection can be traded for transactional proficiency. It is important to take time to build the relationship, establish trust and rapport.

Check logistics before the coaching session: dial-in info, good connections, quality sound system, camera, screen sharing. Check lighting, natural light is 'kinder' than artificial light (ages, shadows under eyes).

As a coach, be aware of camera angle and potential for seeing less body language signals. Agree time to suit if on different time zones.

During the Covid-19 pandemic in early 2020, I did a lot of coaching by digital means. I quickly realised there were a number of tactics that helped me work more effectively during these digitally focused days. I found it beneficial to mix up my schedules, rather than start each day at the same time. There were days when I exercised before starting work, other days I took a longer lunch break and went out for a walk, and other days when I interspersed coaching with administrative chores and creative processes such as writing, reading articles, and spending time on research. Each person has their own preference, and one pattern I noticed when talking to coachees and colleagues was that during the first few days of working remotely, people found productivity and enthusiasm high. This quickly diminished, however. Research by Buffer.com indicated that 'many remote workers struggle with unplugging from their work, loneliness and communicating' ('State of Remote Work 2019', 2020).

Due to the Covid-19 pandemic, there has been a significant shift to coaching by virtual means. Coaching by virtual means can contribute to a better work/life balance, as it is a more efficient use of time for both coach and coachees. While research (Geissler, Hasenbein, Kanatouri & Wegner, 2014) suggests that a coachee can have an impactful experience if the session takes place remotely, certain topics such as behavioural issues are better explored in person. In a digital world, the value of human connection can be traded for transactional proficiency. Through virtual means, we increase touchpoints and yet we can simultaneously lose touch.

 A coachee I was working with me told me about a behavioural issue they had to raise with an employee. Due to Covid-19 restrictions, the conversation took place over the phone. Despite the coachee's best endeavours to handle the issue sensitively, the conversation did not go according to plan and ended up negatively. He felt that in a face-to-face situation the outcome would have been different. In the absence of face-to-face communications, that all-important transfer of trust and authentic good intentions can get lost in translation. It is also important to be aware that working by virtual means engages different parts of the brain than when communicating face-to-face. The impact of eye-contact, loss of certain body language signals and tonality can land differently across a camera. This can place extra demands on energy levels.

During occasions when I have coached or delivered training/facilitation for a full day by virtual means I have been aware of the need to take good breaks in between sessions, shortening the duration of sessions, and having more frequent sessions with each coachee. From the point of managing my own personal energy and making sure I give the best possible support to my coachees, I avoid scheduling multiple successive days coaching and facilitating by virtual means if possible. For me, if coaching is to take place virtually, I prefer to do so by what I call 'hybrid' means: ideally do the first session face-to-face. That said, if the coach/coachee fit is correct regardless of the setting a skilled coach will make the process of coaching look effortless and like a natural conversation, albeit with an effective framework.

Summary of Listening and Communications

- Minimise distractions

- Connect and build rapport (eye-contact, body posture, facial expressions, breathing, energy levels)

- Paraphrase what the coachee says. Observe tone and pitch of voice. Observe physical characteristics. Show empathy

- Be aware of what's not said – changes in body posture, silences, hesitancies. Summarise, clarify, and reflect back the key words

- Control the process (use a well-structured coaching model)

Avoid:

- Talking too much

- Thinking about the next question

- Giving advice, ideas, solutions, or suggestions

- Making assumptions and judgements

Chapter 6: How the mind works, Belief Systems and Values

'Change your thoughts and you change the world' – *Norman Vincent Peale*

In this chapter you will:

- Learn about the neuropsychology of the brain
- Examine the differences between empowering and disempowering beliefs
- Learn a methodology for changing a belief system
- Learn about Value Systems

How the mind works

The works and writings of many leading research psychologists including Brown and Brown in *Neuropsychology for Coaches* (Brown & Brown, 2012), Chamine in *Positive Intelligence*, (Chamine, 2016), Dispenza in *You Are The Placebo* (Dispenza, 2014), Kahneman and Egan (Kahneman & Egan, 2011) in *Thinking Fast and Slow* and the many experts on emotional intelligence such as Dr M Newman (Newman, 2009), Dr D Goleman (Goleman, 2006), Dr S Stein and Dr H Book (Stein & Book, 2011), explore the links between positive intelligence, positive psychology, behavioural science, neural psychology, and performance science. Within us all there are multiple forces at work that vie for control over our mind. In my training I describe these forces as the software of our brain. Our brain represents the hardware, the outer shell of the computer. The neurology of the brain is the software. Depending on the quality of our software, certain outcomes are achieved. This software is influenced by both genetic and inherited factors and by our innate personality, environment, and upbringing.

From the moment you are born, to the first thirty-six hours of your life, you learn to habituate i.e. to not pay attention to anything that is no longer novel. Research shows that infants pay attention to novel and interesting stimuli. Over time they become accustomed to their environment and pay less attention to it. This process is called habituation. When something new happens they once again become alert to their environment and pay attention again. This process is called dishabituation (Developmental Psychology. *Habituation: Studying Infants Before They Can Talk*. JoVE, 2020). From this early age, we are already beginning to set down memories and markers of how our world works.

By the time you are eighteen months old, you have learned to categorise all new people and events. As a result, it takes you just four seconds to form a first impression of anyone or anything new that you encounter.

By the time you are thirty-six months old you have learned the basics of who you think you are, what you are capable and incapable of and what your outlook on life will be. This learning takes place through taking psychological snapshots of events that made a significant impression upon you. The sum total of these snapshots becomes your 'stored knowledge'. By the time you are six years old, 50% of your brain's neural connections die through lack of use.

So, based on our stored data, and on the learning curve we have been on since we were thirty-six hours old, we develop an image of ourselves and our world around us. We translate this into approximately 60,000 thoughts every day, and every day we repeat 90% to 95% of these 60,000 thoughts (Dispenza, 2014). Reflect for yourself how many of these thoughts are Automatic Negative Thoughts (ANTS).

Reflective Exercise

For one day make a mental or written note or use some other means to document all your thoughts and habitual responses. What are your judgements, thought patterns, assumptions, and biases? How many positive vs negative messages do you give yourself?

> *'The mind is in its own place, and in itself can make a heaven of hell, a hell of heaven'* – John Milton

Scientists hooked up a person's brain to a PET scan (Positron Emission Tomography – an imaging technique which produces a three-dimensional image or map of functional processes in the body) and showed the person an object. Certain parts of the brain lit up. If the person was asked to close their eyes and imagine the same object it caused the same part of the brain to light up as when it was looking directly at it. This prompted scientists to ask, 'What is reality – do we see with our brain or do we see with our eyes?'

The brain does not know the difference between what it sees in its environment and what it remembers. Therefore, we live our past experiences as if they are in the present and often find our reactions in our current life being ruled by past events. We fail to differentiate between our past lives and current experiences. (Merrick et al., 2017).

Case Study:

Jane's mother was a dysfunctional, manipulative, and controlling person who used mentally and physically abusive tactics to try to control her environment. Through the collaborative coaching process and the use of a positive intelligence assessment (https://assessment.positiveintelligence.com/saboteur/overview - thank you to Positiveintelligence.com) Jane became aware that when she met a controlling person the past experiences of her mother's behaviour triggered certain reactions and beliefs in herself. Her belief was that what she did was never good enough, the outcome was low self-esteem and a need to always prove herself, a dogged and unhealthy determination and a tendency towards being a hyper achiever and being a people pleaser. Her constant challenge is to be aware of her beliefs and differentiate between what is happening in her present life and the triggers from her past life that she reacts to.

Through our work together and using the positive intelligence programme, Jane took back control of her responses and changed her mindset and belief system about herself.

Regardless of the quality of the parenting we received, we are all triggered in some way and respond to past experiences. We all see our present through a filter of our past and even when we are aware of our triggers, we struggle with separating ourselves from our history. As a coach, we are not qualified to work with remediating past trauma. However, we can work with a coachee to create an awareness of the reason behind their behaviours. A person cannot change what they are not aware of, so opening up a collaborative discussion about a coachee's triggers and reactions can be powerful for the coachee to begin to identify, name, and alter maladaptive responses.

During my years of working with coachees, I realise that people have different ways of processing information. I have found that working with a coachee to understand what their preferred way is of beginning to change those maladaptive, undesirable behaviours and put in place a self-directed strategy, is fundamental to the collaborative approach.

When a coachce designs the strategy, they are more likely to take ownership of and responsibility for its implementation. Some people will write a plan on a spreadsheet, others will carry an image in their minds, others will journal, reflect, and write about it, others may design a vision board, create a mind map or do a brainstorming session – there is no correct method. It is up to coach and coachee to co-design the best way forward and for the coach, through questioning and challenging to support them in clarifying what works best for them. In essence we work with the coachee to understand that the only thing they can control is their own behaviour and how they respond to their environment.

The coachee may get frustrated because they want control of their environment. However, in striving for control in their lives, they miss the point and, in the process, fail to take control of the one and only thing over which they can exercise total and absolute control – their own state of mind. Coming back to the analogy of our brain being like a computer, by taking steps – by deliberately and consciously developing our ability to focus or pay attention to the present – we can take control of our state of mind (the software of the computer) and rewire our brain to change our internal narrative and consequent behaviours.

Research by Wollett and Maguire (Woollett & Maguire, 2011) found the human brain exhibits high plasticity – its shape morphs with use.

The average London Black Cab driver's hippocampus – that part of the brain where we store spatial knowledge and memory – is 50% larger than normal because of 'The Knowledge'. The cab drivers have enhanced the capacity of their brain to remember every road, twist, and turn of the London streets where they drive without the use of maps or GPS systems. A professional violinists' right motor cortex is larger than average because of their coordinated left-hand movements. These findings point to the brain's ability to mould its wiring, structure, and even size to the use to which it is put.

Research has confirmed that stem cells are present in the adult central nervous system. In other words, the adult brain grows completely new neurons according to our usage requirements. You can physically rewire your brain by consistently using it in a different way. By doing small things differently you can break habitual behavioural patterns and, quite literally, change your responses and behaviours. If you expect something different, something different will happen. Dr M Maltz (Maltz & Powers, 2010), a plastic surgeon, observed that it took patients twenty-one days to stop phantom sensations in their limbs post-amputation. Through research, he concluded it takes this amount of time for new neural pathways to be formed and old ones to atrophy and therefore, he suggested, old habits can be broken and new ones established in this time frame. More recent research suggests it takes between 66 and 254 days to change a habit. Although the brain is not a muscle, this process is similar to building muscle in the brain. *As a coach we can collaborate with the coachee to cultivate a mindset of goal setting and focus to achieve this re-wiring of the brain.* My own personal experience of achieving personal change and supporting coachees in making change is the need to constantly practise and embed new behaviours. Like exercising, if we do not continue to focus on maintaining the new habits, behaviours, and thought processes, the inner critic, those 60,000 daily thoughts, those old laid-down behaviours will revert to original form and we will continue to self-sabotage. In his book *Positive Intelligence*, Shirzad Chamine explores how we can work with both ourselves and a coachee to rewire the brain and diminish the impact of the negative thoughts (Chamine refers to these negative thoughts as Saboteurs). (Chamine, 2016).

Through the collaborative coaching process, the coach can work with the coachee to maintain focus and effect change. Focus matters, the coach can explore with the coachee ways to develop their mental focus, commitment, and determination.

Reflective Exercise

How can a coach support a coachee to dismantle habitual thought patterns and behaviours?

One option is to work with the coachee to start by changing small habitual behaviours or thoughts. How can the coach collaboratively co-design with the coachee a strategy and tactics to achieve this? For some this might involve making a 21-day plan which includes writing a reminder each day in a journal or electronic diary or seeking the support of a trusted friend to whom you are accountable (see Appendix 2), for others it might be becoming aware of self-talk and start each day with a reminder of how they want to control their judgements, thought processes and mental computer software. During the day the coachee can check in with how their clarity of mind compares to the clarity of mind they feel at the start of the day.

For some coachees it might help them to create a physical action such as pinching a thumb and finger together each time they become aware of a negative thought; this action is called an 'anchor' and creates an external response (pinching two fingers together) to an internal event such as a negative thought. The outcome is that a person heightens their awareness of their thought processes or habits. Working with the coachee to find a strategy and range of tactics that works for the coachee is fundamental to success. I have worked with some coachees who will combine a number of different options and tactics to achieve success, others prefer to limit the interventions, there is no 'must do' or perfect solution.

The more experienced a coach becomes, the more they will develop a range of techniques, skills, and tools and develop the courage to give the power to the coachee to choose what works best for them.

Belief Systems

The magic of belief systems

> What you believe to be true, you create to be true! In the words of Henry Ford, 'whether you believe you can or you believe you can't, you're right'.

Reflective Exercise

Recall five things you used to believe – but no longer do! What was your belief system about Santa? What was your belief system about friends, family, life, fun, security when you were under ten years of age, twenty-five years of age, forty years of age and so on?

Recall five things that you firmly believe in now.

> What is your conclusion from this reflection?

Understanding our belief systems

When something happens for the first time, it happens because somebody somewhere believed it could happen; the belief always precedes the event. The first under-four-minute-mile runner, Roger Bannister, empowered hundreds of other runners to believe that such a feat was possible. Consequently, other runners achieved the same result following Bannister's achievement.

Every object in the world commenced as a thought, as an idea. It must happen in your mind before it happens in your world. Remember, it is impossible to see something that you do not believe is there. It is also impossible to disbelieve in the apparent existence of what you do see.

I remember as a child when I was seven years old, on Christmas Eve, my two brothers showed me our 'Santa' toys that had been hidden by my parents. To the chagrin of our neighbours, I announced to all my friends living on the same road that there was no such thing as Santa. Mary, my best friend at the time, angrily disputed my story. According to her belief system, Santa had visited her and told her she would get a Barbie doll for Christmas. Needless to say, Mary got her Barbie doll, on Christmas morning, definite evidence of her belief system.

How many similar examples can you recall?

If you don't believe that something will happen, it won't. All belief systems contain within them a self-actualising logic and a system of evidence to support it. Our brain filters for information based on the messages we give it.

Most of us take our beliefs for granted. As a coach it can be beneficial to work with a person to examine their beliefs. But tread carefully! You may be pushing the person's boundaries and taking them out of their comfort zone.

Case Study:

A few years ago, I was working with a colleague to train a group to climb Mount Kilimanjaro in Africa. My colleague worked on physical fitness and stamina with the group and I worked with the group to help them develop their mental resilience. One day a lady, let's call her Fiona, approached me. She was sixty-five years of age and asked if I thought she would be capable of climbing the mountain. I explored this question with her. What were the boundaries she was putting on herself? What limiting beliefs were holding her back? What would she say to a friend of a similar age who asked her if she thought they would be capable of climbing Kilimanjaro? Through this collaborative coaching conversation she answered the question for herself. She realised that fear of failure was holding her back. She realised that all limiting beliefs stem from some kind of fear.

Understanding empowering and disempowering beliefs

A belief is a generalisation about what may happen – a guiding principle.

They help us make sense of the world and give coherence to our experience. Beliefs help us protect the present and navigate the future. There are beliefs that empower you and give you choice and open possibilities, and of course there are beliefs that disempower you, closing down choice.

Empowering and Disempowering Beliefs

Empowering Beliefs	Disempowering Beliefs
I have just left behind twenty seconds of bad luck or hassle	It's going to be one of those days!
Money can provide me with the means to achieve what I want	Money causes trouble
I can trust myself to choose whom I trust	I can't trust anyone
There are good men/women out there	All men/women are jerks
I can do that	People like me (my age, culture, social background) don't do that

Reflective Exercise

Which type of beliefs would you voluntarily choose?

Let's look at some examples of the way a coachee may programme themselves for failure or success.

> 'I believe that I create my own success!'

> 'I do not believe that I create my own success!'

> What will the former belief produce in your life?

> What will the latter belief produce in your life?

As a coach you will find that the world your clients have created is the product of their beliefs, and almost certainly they will never have examined or even thought about those 'certainties' on which they base the existence of those beliefs. The role of the collaborative coach, through skills such as powerful questioning techniques, is to work with the coachee to find a way to change their mind and create a shift for themselves. It is essential for a coachee to identify and understand their underlying beliefs.

Beliefs are often expressed as 'should', 'oughts', and 'musts': 'I have to...' 'I can't...' 'I shouldn't...' 'I must...'

They are inaction words. As a coach, a powerful question is to ask 'Whose should is it?' 'Who says you can't?'

Examples of self-limiting beliefs are: 'I can't do that'; 'I'm not good enough'

'I shouldn't take time out because it is a selfish thing to do'

'I always have to be nice to...'

By asking simple and effective questions we can support a coachee in achieving a shift in their belief system.

As a coach, it is important to understand the nature and structure of belief systems. Beliefs are intangible and frequently unconscious. They are often confused with facts. A fact is based on something that has happened, whereas a belief is a generalisation about what will happen. Some of our beliefs give us freedom, choice, and open possibilities.

How are Beliefs formed?

Beliefs may be:

- Formed haphazardly from meaning we deduced from our day-to-day experiences.

- Handed to us by the beliefs and modes of thinking learned from our parents, teachers, environment, the mass-media, authority figures of all kinds, and society in general. As a youngster, you probably accepted those earlier, handed-down beliefs without question. You were not even aware that you had a choice. You then engraved those beliefs on your mind and they became real for you.

- Formed from a sudden unexpected conflict, trauma or confusion and the younger we are the more likely this is to happen.

- Formed from repetition – the experience has no emotional intensity, it just keeps happening – like water drip, drip, dripping.

- Based on fact and may be true: the world is round.

All beliefs are real for the believer.

Reflective Exercise

Beliefs can control and drive our behaviour. What do you believe about this statement?

How can a coach work with a coachee to change a belief?

Changing a belief requires changing the subconscious program, since a belief is a subconscious state of being. Beliefs are thoughts and feelings that you keep thinking over and over again until you hardwire them into your brain and emotionally condition them into your body. You could say you become addicted to your beliefs, which is why it is so hard to change them and is why it doesn't feel good on a gut level when they are challenged.

You have certainly changed your beliefs in the past. Which of us still believes all the things we believed when we were five years old? When you change a belief, replace it with an empowering one that honours the positive intention of your former belief. In addition, the new belief must be congruent with your sense of self.

There are several ways to work with a coachee to begin to change a belief (often called Belief Transformation Exercises). One process to change a belief is described in the following steps:

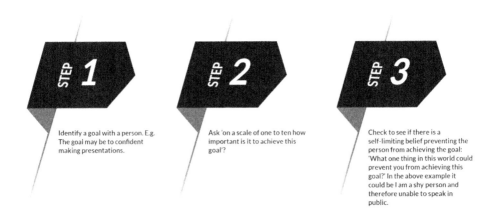

First, as a coach, clearly identify and acknowledge with the coachee the limiting beliefs that they currently hold.

Step 1

Identify a goal with a person – such a goal may be to become more comfortable making a presentation.

Step 2

Ask 'on a scale of one to ten how important is it to achieve this goal?'

Step 3

Check to see if there is a self-limiting belief preventing the person from achieving the goal: 'What one thing in this world could prevent you from achieving this goal?' The self-limiting belief could be 'I am a shy person and therefore unable to speak in public'.

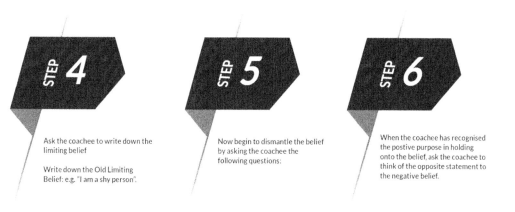

Step 4

Ask the coachee to write down the limiting belief.

Write down the Old Limiting Belief: e.g. 'I am a shy person'.

Step 5

Now begin to dismantle the belief by asking the coachee the following questions:

What assumptions are you making about yourself e.g. the coachee may assume that they are not good enough because they have never achieved this before.

What generalisations are they making about themselves (e.g. shy people can't speak in public)?

Ask coachee for one instance in their past life of when they spoke in front of other people – just one example, and then challenge by saying 'so you have never, ever, ever spoken in public before, not once?'

Then follow up with questions such as 'and what was the worst outcome from this experience?'

Ask coachee to look for evidence of how they have achieved in other areas of their lives and help them to build on and recognise past success and that they are a capable and competent person.

Ask 'What is holding onto this belief doing for you? What fear is behind the belief?'

How is this belief keeping them stuck?

How is the belief serving them? What is the payoff/positive purpose of holding onto this belief?

I have found when I drill down on my questioning and ask the coachee what is the payoff/positive purpose of holding onto this belief, most answer that there is no positive purpose. The role of the coach at this point is to continue to push the coachee through questioning techniques, to realise that there is a positive purpose or benefit to holding onto the belief. The breakthrough moment in this exercise is for the coachee to realise that the positive purpose for holding onto the belief is that it is in some way protecting them. So in the case of being shy, the positive purpose could be protecting them from the fear of rejection or the fear of failure, or some other fear.

Step 6

When the coachee has recognised the positive purpose in holding onto the belief, ask the coachee to think of the opposite statement to the negative belief. One way of doing this is to use what we call an incisive questioning technique. Incisive questions are in two parts. The first part of the question removes a limiting belief; the second part addresses the goal. So working on our example of a person who is too shy to speak in public ask 'If you knew you were comfortable speaking in public (remove the limiting belief) what would change for you (address the goal)?'

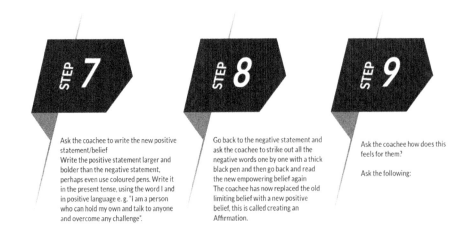

Step 7

Ask the coachee to write the new positive statement/belief.

Write the positive statement larger and bolder than the negative statement, perhaps even use coloured pens.

Write it in the present tense, using the word *I* and in positive language e. g. 'I am a person who is comfortable speaking in public and who is able to hold my own, talk to anyone and speak with composure and confidence'.

Step 8

Go back to the negative statement and ask the coachee to strike out all the negative words one by one with a thick black pen and then go back and read the new empowering belief again.

The coachee has now replaced the old limiting belief with a new positive belief. This is called creating an Affirmation.

Step 9

Ask the coachee how does this feel for them?

Ask the following:

How might your life be better with a new empowering belief?

How might life be worse with this new belief?

What is the best thing that could possibly happen if you embrace the proposed new belief?

Ask which belief do they want to hold onto: the old limiting belief or the new empowering one?

The coachee should feel connected to and believe in the new belief.

Affirmations

When you have found a new empowering belief, write down the new empowering belief as an affirmation. The affirmation should be written in the present, personal tense e.g. 'I believe I can do anything I wish with great results'.

When forming affirmations, the coach supports the coachee to:

Compose and write the affirmation.

Check that the new affirmation is congruent with the coachee's values and that the coachee takes ownership of the statement.

The coachee should state the new affirmation as often as possible for **at least twenty-one days**, starting in the morning when they wake up and before going to sleep at night. This helps to rewire and change the neural pathway in the brain (my personal belief is that changing the neural pathways in the brain takes longer than twenty-one days. When working with clients I suggest that they need to focus on the change for at least seven weeks and be aware of the need for ongoing maintenance far beyond this timeline). The power of using an affirmation is it can be called up as we go about our everyday life.

When working on beliefs, it is important to understand the connection between our beliefs, our emotions, and our thoughts.

Let's consider as an example the symbol of a three-sided prism; the prism represents *you*. Consider the sides of the prism as being the

following:

A belief generates an emotion; both together generate thoughts, which in turn precipitate action. As an example, right now, take a few moments to clarify what you believe about any particular thing. Now, choose another belief which you would prefer to hold about that same thing.

Beliefs are truly powerful constructs. Remember, all the coaching in the world will not bring a client to achieve a goal if they don't believe they can achieve it!

The area of health shows us how powerful beliefs truly are. A one-sentence pronouncement from a medical doctor can in effect become a death sentence. This 'placebo effect' is another example of the power of belief; the brain can convince the body that a fake treatment is working.

Everything that you believe, and hold dearly, is based essentially on a belief system. The stronger you hold a belief system, the stronger it holds you, and reduces your range of choices. Sometimes, we hold onto a belief because we have simply unquestioningly accepted or inherited that belief. As a coach we can ask the coachee, what is prompting this belief?

Are they prepared to be less rigid in their beliefs, perhaps to be open to the possibility that there is a different belief that may serve them better?

Values and fulfilment

A value is something that is important to us, it is an invisible force that influences the way we live our lives. They influence what is a priority to us and guide us in the decisions we make. Many people have never thought about their values.

The link between values and fulfilment is so obvious it may be invisible. Helping a coachee discover and clarify their values is a way to create a map that will guide them through the decision paths of their lives. When a coachee clarifies their values, they learn more about what makes them tick, and what is important for them and what is not. When we work collaboratively with coachees on this topic, they discover what is truly essential to them in their lives. It helps them take a stand and make choices based on what is fulfilling to them. Honouring one's values is inherently fulfilling even when it is difficult. When the value is not being honoured, a person feels internal tension. The price is a sense of selling out on oneself – and the result is an unfulfilling life – a life of toleration rather than fulfilment.

Values drive our behaviour:

Values are described as the 'Hot Buttons' that drive our behaviour. They are unconscious motivators or de-motivators. Depending on the values we choose, they can move us towards or away from where we want to go. If I want to be a generous, giving person but fear scarcity more than I value abundance and giving, my value system of scarcity will contradict what I want to move towards. My values need to support my goals. Values are a reference point by which to judge whether actions and behaviours are creating a sense of 'rightness', or congruence, in our lives.

Values are influenced by different life stages – what is important to us when we are twenty years of age is different to what we prioritise at fifty years of age.

These priorities arise as a result of:

- The individual's personal need to change
- The need to meet different social and economic demands

According to research into adult development, during our life we go through different life stages. One theory by Levinson (Levinson, 1986), suggests that during these stages we move from a transition stage where we rebuild our life structure and enhance our lives, to a stable stage where we consolidate, build on, and cope with changes made during the transition stage. Different life stages will influence our value system. I have worked with many coachees whose value system in their early 20s is connected to their career and progressing up the corporate ladder. As they move into their 30s and early 40s, they may experience a shift into the settling down phase of life where starting a family, establishing a niche in society or reflecting on life goals may cause them to question their value system around work vs family, community, and leisure.

When working with a person's value system, it is important to recognise that there is a difference between values and morals or principles. I may have a value system around providing for my family, however the morality of how I do this e.g. through criminal activity, may seem contradictory. As a coach we may be challenged by a coachee's value systems and morality.

Reflective Exercise

How would you manage yourself when working with a person whose value system or moral compass differs from yours?

Values Are Who We Are:

When we honour our values, there's a sense of internal 'rightness'. As a coach you want to know what is in the coachee's heart and help them understand what is important for them. You are much less concerned about a dictionary definition of values than the coachee's definition. The wording must work for them.

It is worth explaining to a coachee that values are intangible; they are not something we do or have. Money, for example, is not a value. Travel is not a value. Gardening is not a value.

The value is the intangible return that causes us to place a level of importance on these items. Money may represent a value around freedom or independence or security depending on what is important to the individual. Very often our values are linked to emotions – security may evoke an emotion of happiness or feeling of freedom.

As a coach we should also be aware that there are different type of values.

Karin Miller (Miller, 2015) describes ten global values – unity; community; life; freedom; connection; sustainability; creativity; empowerment; choice; and integrity. Others suggest global values are generic values we all share such as peace and harmony, and core values – career, friends, family, health. However you choose to describe values, our values are connected to one of the following basic needs:

- Identity – each of us needs to know who we are
- Connection – each of us has a need for love and to feel part of a group to feel attached to another person
- Impact – each of us needs to feel that we make a contribution of some sort and has an impact on the environment and people around us
- Stability – each of us feels the need to have a place of security and privacy to which we can retreat

The process of satisfying these needs in our lives helps us to define and understand our value systems. When goal setting with a coachee, the coach should check with the coachee that their goals are congruent with their value system. During a coaching session it may become apparent that a goal is inconsistent with a coachee's value system. A coach may therefore have to challenge a coachee about alignment between goals and values. Each of us assigns different levels of importance to different values and, as already discussed, our value system will vary depending on various factors, including our life stage. Part of the work of the coach is to help a coachee recognise and prioritise their value system. Knowing the order or hierarchy of your value system empowers a person to stay focused and motivated and to set goals that are congruent with their value system. In a collaborative conversation, the coach and coachee work together to co-design a hierarchy of values. One way to do this is to encourage the coachee to make a list of their values.

STEP 1 — Ask the coachee to choose their top ten values.

STEP 2 — Ask the coachee to prioritise their values, ranking the top ten from highest to lowest. The highest value No 1 might be love the 10th highest value might be success.

STEP 3 — Ask the coachee to eliminate values until they are left with three top values.

Step 1. Ask the coachee to choose their top ten values. (One way to do this is to ask them to use the list of values in Appendix 4 as a prompt.)

In addition to the above, you can ask the coachee to name the most important people in their lives – these people may be family members, friends, colleagues, people they are familiar with from the bigger global world such as high-profile leaders, gurus, characters from a film, or other fictional characters.

When they have identified a number of these people, ask them what the characteristic is they identify with each of these people. Ask them to name a different characteristic for each person. The characteristic they choose normally reflects a value that is important to them, the coachee. When I have worked with people on this topic, people may choose a parent because of the love they have shown, or a guru such as Gandhi or Nelson Mandela because of their integrity, or a fictional character in a movie that reflects something that is important for them to have, be it happiness, success, wealth, health, or fitness.

The list of ten characteristics then becomes a list of their ten top values. The list can be longer or shorter than ten; the important thing is for the coachee to begin to understand their values.

Step 2 Ask the coachee to prioritise their values, ranking the top ten from highest to lowest. The highest value might be love, the lowest value might be success.

Step 3 Ask the coachee to eliminate values until they are left with three top values. The reason for this is a person cannot make a decision based on their ten top values, therefore they need to clarify for themselves what values are most important to them.

The main result in this exercise is not the finished priority list – the coachee is free to change the order on the list any time. The real importance is that it forces the coachee to see the value itself beyond the word. If the coachee has chosen the value of security as their highest value, explore with the coachee what the word security means to them? By ranking the order of their values, the person must consider one value over the other and consider how living to this value will influence the decisions and choices they make.

When the coachee has completed the exercise, ask how they are honouring those values on a scale of one to ten, where one means the value is not being honoured in their lives, and ten means it is honoured completely all of the time. Is the value an aspirational one, or a true value that is lived and guides how they make decisions?

There are almost certain to be values that are ranked at four, five or six which are of importance to the coachee and which the coachee may feel are getting 'squashed' or compromised. The balancing act of your life may mean living with a certain amount of compromise – perhaps the job you do is pretty soulless but the money it gives you supports your value of security, which may have a higher priority for you at certain times of your life. There are almost certain to be values that are not being honoured and may be causing internal tension or resentment. When we are honouring our values, they become the benchmark by which we live our lives.

Powerful questions a coach can ask are:

- 'What is the price you pay for not honouring that value?'
- 'What's stopping you?'
- 'If you make this decision, what value will you have honoured?'

Making decisions based on one's top values will always lead to a more fulfilling decision. It may not be the easiest, or the most enjoyable or the most fun, but it will be the most fulfilling. Sometimes the most radical change in life that can be made is deciding to be truly authentic. When you rank your values, you clarify what is most important to you.

Case Study:

Cathy had been appointed to the Senior Executive Leadership Team in a fast-paced multinational finance company. Her track record over the years had been stellar and she was sponsored by her company to complete an executive development programme that would prepare her for an appointment to the Board of Directors. Similar to many executives at this level, she lacked confidence in her ability to perform successfully at board level. At first she thought it was this fear of failure that was holding her back, however, through a collaborative coaching process and by looking at all the aspects of what was holding her back she realised that work/life balance was more important to her than moving to the next level.

Similar to the role of values in our personal life, values in the corporate world influence goal setting; they create a vision and common purpose. In an organisation, having clear company values sets a common understanding for employees, creates greater commitment, and is like the DNA of an organisation. When a company lives its values, as opposed to having aspirational values, it builds trust and cohesiveness. Values are like a compass that motivates and guides, and helps employees and key stakeholders understand an organisation's purpose and what it stands for. It is a constant that guides employees in decision making, developing strategy, and achieving the company's vision and goals.

In a volatile, constantly changing environment where uncertainty is the norm, clear company values are like a map that aligns employees and key stakeholders with strategic direction. If, for example, integrity is one of a company's values, the company must first define what the word integrity means. It then needs to clarify the relevance of integrity to its business needs and strategy. The outcome might be a statement that 'integrity is critical to our company because it underpins how we collaborate with other key stakeholders and business partners'. An effective exercise for the Senior Leadership Team could be to imagine if they were an important client. How, then, would they like to see the company conduct its business in a commercially effective and honourable way? Similar to personal values, a company can identify its top values and then align those values with its company policies, strategy, customer and employee interactions. These values can be embodied and set out in the company's mission statement.

Chapter 7: Concluding Coaching

'Life begins at the end of your comfort zone' – Neale Donald Walshe, Author

In this chapter, we will look at the topic of concluding the coaching contract or the coaching sessions.

Concluding coaching

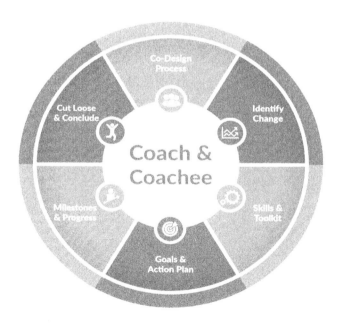

How do you know when the time is right?

The completion of a coaching contract will evolve in different ways. In many contracts, particularly in Executive/Business Coaching, a specific number of sessions may be agreed at the contracting phase. This may be extended through agreement between all the relevant parties to the original contract. On the other hand, like facets of coaching, it may evolve from the intuitive process. There is an underlying sense that the coaching sessions have run their course. However, it is necessary to check that coach and coachee have reached the same point in the process.

In this situation, the first step to concluding coaching is to find out if the coachee is comfortable that the coaching is coming to an end.

Revisit the original goals – refer to the Intake Session, Original Assessment and any notes you made during the course of the coaching contract.

What was the purpose of the coachee coming to you?

What issue did the coachee present with at the first session?

Did the coachee complete a Life Wheel or Executive/Business Wheel?

Examine the changes.

What other issues presented?

Have these been dealt with?

Some powerful questions:

What benefits has the coachee got from the coaching?

What is the purpose of this question?

To establish the benefit of the coachee's commitment to coaching.

These benefits are not just goal- or task-based, but also reflect on growth, development, behavioural change, and insights into different aspects of their lives.

What actions will they start and maintain as a result of the coaching?

What is the return for effort put into coaching?

What are the effects of coaching conversations & action plans on the coachee's life (work, home, relationships)?

It may be worth asking:

- 'If you hadn't had the coaching what would be different now?'
- 'If you continue with new behaviours & routines, how will the future be?'

Purpose of completion

The purpose of a formal wrap up and completion is to:

- Leave the coachee feeling that the coaching has been worthwhile.

- Review Client's Future Visions/Plans. Help coachee design a Personal Development Plan. Depending on the coachee's preferred learning style, this could be agreeing a reading list, ongoing self-development through relevant online and digital media resources, attending workshops, networking, or keeping a reflective journal.

- Review what has worked – Express Confidence! Coaching is about making change. Successful coaching leads to self-empowerment. Discuss future success. It is reached by staying committed to the destination and being flexible about the journey. Reflect to the coachee the progress and steps you have witnessed and seek their feedback on what has worked for them.

- Make sure the individual feels supported; it may be appropriate to suggest that the door is always open if future support is needed.

What are the emotions attached to concluding coaching?

At the outset, the role of the coach is to build rapport, trust, and intimacy with a coachee. Some coachees may experience a loss at the end of a series of coaching sessions. This may result from current life circumstances, disillusionment with their working environment, or other unresolved challenges. If as a coach you think this may be an issue it is worth exploring the loss/grief cycle with the coachee.

Elisabeth Kubler-Ross developed a theory that suggested that there are five stages in the grief process. The five stages – Denial, Anger, Bargaining/Fantasy, Depression, Acceptance – are part of a framework that helps people understand the emotions they are experiencing during a time of loss. The model has been adapted into the business world to help people understand the impact of change on them. Not everyone goes through all the stages, nor is it a linear process where a person cycles through each stage one after the other. For each person, moving on and embedding change is a unique process that is shaped by many factors such as childhood experiences, traumatic events, and genetic inheritance. David Kessler who co-authored a book with Kubler-Ross, suggests a sixth stage of grief: 'Finding Meaning'. Kessler's journey with grief started through a traumatic childhood event when he experienced a mass shooting at a time when his mother was dying. His life was further upended by the unexpected death of his twenty-one-year-old son. His book on the sixth stage of grief, 'Finding Meaning', shares his insights.

On occasions a person may feel a sense of loss at the end of a series of coaching sessions. However, the normal outcome from the coaching is that the coachee feels empowered, motivated, and has gained new insights and energy from the coaching. Your role as the coach is to tune into what is needed to achieve effective closure so that the coachee will draw meaning from the sessions with you. The coachee may need reflective space to embed and consolidate their thinking or they may need action and momentum. A coach should act like an energiser that supports the coachee in moving forward independently and with confidence.

Summary

As described at the start of the book Coaching is 'A safe place but also a transitional space where the coachee moves out of their safe place.'
– Kets De Vries

This book is a first step in learning and understanding the coaching process. I hope it has given you an understanding that, to develop a collaborative coaching relationship, the coach has to be comfortable trusting that the coachee is a fully functioning person who is capable of finding solutions that are right for them. To change behaviour, the coachee has to change their awareness of themselves and find solutions to problematic issues. The coach, throughout the coaching process, gives the coachee the means and awareness to support themselves more effectively. It is this awareness process that ultimately creates and supports change and places responsibility for success (whatever that means to the coachee) in the hands of the coachee.

Appendix 1

Business Terms

Business Term	Explanation
Profit	Money earned, after expenses are subtracted from revenue. The excess of selling price over all costs and expenses incurred in making a sale.
Profit Margin	The ratio of the net profit of an organisation to its turnover: at its simplest, its profit expressed as a percentage of sales.
Benchmark	A measurement or standard that serves as a point of reference by which performance, usually process performance, is measured. It involves identifying the best practices from industry and government, and comparing and adapting them to the organisation's operations. The idea is to identify more efficient and effective processes for achieving intended results, and suggesting ambitious goals for program output, product or service quality and process improvement.
Business Case	A structured proposal for business improvement that functions as a decision package for organisational decision-makers. A business case includes an analysis of business process performance and associated needs or

	problems, proposed alternative solutions, assumptions and constraints and a risk-adjusted cost-benefit analysis.
Cash Flow	The transfer of money into and out of an enterprise. It is the flow of cash into a company in the form of revenues, and out of the company in the form of expenses.
Core capability	A specific set of organisational competencies that give an organisation a sustainable competitive advantage. It might be skills, information bases, managerial systems, compelling values or the organisation's tangible assets – things that together create a special advantage for an organisation.
Human Capital	The skills and knowledge possessed by the workforce that have been acquired through formal education and on-the-job and life experience.
Intangible benefit	Benefits (produced by an investment) that are not obvious or measurable.
Market Share	The percentage of the total sales of a given type of product or service that is attributable to a given company.
Organisational DNA	The term 'organisational DNA' was coined as a metaphor for the collection of traits that characterises different organisations. The concept originated from a desire to distil years of experience about the factors that

	differentiate successful companies from their competitors.
Outsourcing	The contracting out to an external provider, work that was previously done within the organisation – it could be a service function (customer services), a manufacturing process or an internal function (accounting).
Stakeholder	An individual or group of individuals with an interest in the success of an organisation in delivering its intended results and in maintaining the viability of the organisation's products and services. Stakeholders influence programmes, products and services.
Strategic Plan	This plan documents who an organisation is, where they are going and how they are going to get there. It is a documented forward-looking plan that aims to map out the means to achieve longer-term goals and to plan a response to unforeseen problems and opportunities.
Target Audience	Audience to whom an organisation's advertising is directed. The target audience is defined in terms of demographic characteristics such as age, sex, ethnicity, education, income, buying habits and more.

TLA's (Three Letter Acronyms)

Business TLA	Explanation
BPR	Business Process Re-engineering – improving efficiency of the business process. Looking at processes from a 'clean slate' perspective
CEO	Chief Executive Officer
CFO	Chief Financial Officer
CRM	Customer Relationship Management
ERP	Enterprise Resource Planning
FIFO	First in first out (or Fit In or F*** Off!)
KPI	Key Performance Indicator
MBO	Management by Objectives
NMJ	Not My Job
ROI	Return on Investment
SAT	Sales Accelerated Technology
SBU	Special/Strategic Business Unit
TKO	Total Knock-out
TQM	Total Quality Management

Appendix 2 – 21-Day Planning Exercise

The exercise can be completed by yourself or by enlisting the support of a trusted friend to whom you will be accountable.

Think about the last twelve months and recall one goal, task or behaviour that you feel proud to have accomplished.

Now complete the following steps:

Step 1

How difficult was this for you?

    Very

    Moderately

    Somewhat

    Not Very Difficult

If you did not make any changes in the last year, think of the last change you felt proud of making. How long ago was this?

How difficult was it to achieve this goal, task, or behaviour?

    Very

    Moderately

    Somewhat

    Not Very Difficult

The purpose of the above is to recognise that despite setbacks and challenges you achieved the desired outcome.

Step 2

Identify a new goal, task, or behaviour you wish to achieve. Avoid using the word **not**. **Choose** something you want to start doing instead of something you want to stop, e.g. 'I want to engage in active listening' rather than 'I want to stop interrupting'.

If it is a change in behaviour you wish to achieve, continue on. If it is a goal or task you wish to achieve, jump to Step 3.

Describe your current behaviour What do you do now? E.g. 'I keep interrupting others when they are speaking'.

How do you feel when you act this way?

What is the benefit of keeping the current behaviour or situation? (What might get in the way of making this change in behaviour? Even when we desire the change we are making, there are many 'pulls' to keeping the status quo. Our negative behaviours serve some purpose. They have some benefit to us. Resist judging yourself harshly when this happens to you. Be self-forgiving, compassionate, and personally vigilant).

Step 3

Describe what the benefit is of achieving this goal, task, or change in behaviour. (What do you want to happen as a result of making this change?)

Guidelines for creating your 21-Day rule statement of commitment

Now that you have identified the goal, task, or behaviour on which you wish to focus, you must meet each one of the following guidelines for best results:

Select only one goal, task, or behaviour

Make the change as specific as possible. Keep the description simple and direct, avoid vague statements like, 'I'll be more organised' or 'I'll be more assertive'. Instead, say, 'I'll spend five minutes every day organising my timetable' or 'I will go for a walk at least once every day'.

Be certain that your goal, task or behaviour is measurable so that you can gauge your success.

Declaring your 21-Day rule statement of commitment

You are now ready to draft your 21-Day rule, 'Statement of Commitment'. Using the guidelines, prepare a statement that will work for you and write it below. Example, 'Every day, for twenty-one days, I will ...'

Statement:

Every day for twenty-one days I will:

Before you continue, you must answer the two most important questions.

Q1. On a scale of 1 to 10, how committed are you to this? If the commitment is not high enough for you to really want to do it then stop, go back, and select a change you want to achieve.

YOU MUST WANT TO DO IT!

Q2. Will you take full power and full responsibility for your actions?

Make sure you are doing this for yourself, not for someone else, or to satisfy a list of 'shoulds' or 'ought tos'. When you take full power and full responsibility, you will have the greatest success.

YOU MUST TAKE FULL RESPONSIBILITY AND FULL POWER FOR YOUR ACTIONS

FINAL STATEMENT:

Commitment: Every day for twenty-one days, I will actively pursue this goal, task, or change in behaviour.

(Source Unknown)

Appendix 3 – Sample questions on how to start a coaching session

The coachee may bring a specific topic to a coaching session or the following questions may be of use in discussing different coaching topics outlined on the coaching wheel.

Physical surroundings

How important are your physical surroundings/environment to you? (This can be home or work environment.)

On a scale of one to ten, how comfortable are you with your physical surroundings?

What one improvement would you like to make to your physical surroundings?

What is stopping you from changing your physical surroundings?

Fitness and fun

What does fitness mean to you?

Where on a scale of one to ten are you in your preferred level of fitness?

What one improvement would you like to make to your fitness?

What is stopping you?

What does fun and recreation mean to you?

How many times a day do you smile?

Where on a scale of one to ten are you in fun and recreation?

What pastimes do you find most fulfilling?

What one change would you like to make to your social life?

What is stopping you?

Finance/Money

What does money represent to you? Security? Independence? Acceptance? Success? Status?

How comfortable are you with your financial situation at present?

Where on a scale of one to ten are you at the moment?

What does financial stability mean to you?

How much of a priority is making more money?

Personal development

Where are you in your personal development?

Where on a scale of one to ten are you?

How comfortable are you with your personal growth at the moment?

What is holding you back right now?

What is your biggest fear?

What motivates you to want to improve?

Relationships

What does the word family mean to you? (Note the family questions could be divided between your current family, if you are married or with a partner, and the family you grew up with.)

Who are the important people in your life at the moment?

Where on a scale of one to ten are you with your important relationships?

How important is your family to you?

What one improvement would you like to make in your family relationships?

What role do you play in your family?

Friends:

How important are your friends to you?

How well do you fit in with your friends?

What is the balance between giving and receiving in your relationships?

Skills and toolkit

What skills do you have?

What skills and tools would you like to improve on to help you at work or at home?

Where on a scale of one to ten are you with your skills and tools? How comfortable are you with your current level?

What one improvement would you like to make to your skills?

What resources are you missing that you feel are necessary for your success?

Work and career

How important is your work and career to you?

Where on a scale of one to ten are you in your work and career aspirations? How comfortable are you with this level?

What is the most fulfilling aspect of your work?

How much stress is there in your work?

Where is the stress coming from in your work?

What one thing would you like to change about your work?

What one next step would you like to take in relation to your work?

Well-being

What does well-being mean to you?

How important is well-being to you?

Where on a scale of one to ten are you at the moment?

How comfortable are you with your level of well-being and self-care at the moment?

What recharges your batteries?

How fluid and flexible are you in your lifestyle?

What one change would you like to make to your level of well-being?

What one improvement would you like to make in your quality of life?

Feedback

How beneficial was this exploration to you?

What went well?

What other areas of your life would you like to explore?

Where were you when you first started the coaching process?

Where are you now?

What one thing would you like to do differently the next time we meet? (Source Unknown)

Appendix 4 – List of values

The following **list of values** will help you develop a clearer sense of what's most important to you in life. Mark the values which most resonate with you, and then sort your list in order of priority. As you scan the values list below, you may find that while most values have little or no significance to you (and some may even seem negative to you), there are those values that just jump out and call to you, and you feel 'Yes, this value is part of me'. This values list is merely a guide. It is lengthy though certainly not exhaustive, so feel free to add unlisted values to your own list as well.

List of values

Benevolence	Fascination	Poise Polish
Bliss	Fashion	Popularity
Boldness	Fearlessness	Potency
Bravery	Ferocity	Power
Brilliance	Fidelity	Practicality
Buoyancy	Fierceness	Pragmatism
Calmness	Financial Independence	Precision
Camaraderie	Firmness	Preparedness

Candour	Fitness	Presence
Capability	Flexibility	Privacy
Care	Flow	Proactivity
Carefulness	Fluency	Professionalism
Celebrity	Focus	Prosperity
Certainty	Fortitude	Prudence
Challenge	Frankness	Punctuality
Charity	Freedom	Purity
Charm	Friendliness	Realism
Chastity	Frugality	Reason
Cheerfulness	Fun	Reasonableness
Clarity	Gallantry	Recognition
Cleanliness	Generosity	Recreation
Clear-mindedness	Gentility	Refinement
Cleverness	Giving	Reflection
Closeness	Grace	Relaxation
Comfort	Gratitude	Reliability
Commitment	Gregariousness	Religiousness

Compassion	Growth	Resilience
Completion	Guidance	Resolution
Composure	Happiness	Resolve
Concentration	Harmony Health	Resourcefulness
Confidence	Heart	Respect
Conformity	Helpfulness	Rest
Congruency	Heroism	Restraint
Connection	Holiness	Reverence
Consciousness	Honesty	Richness
Consistency	Honour	Rigour
Contentment	Hopefulness	Sacredness
Continuity	Hospitality	Sacrifice
Contribution	Humility	Sagacity
Control	Humour	Saintliness
Conviction	Hygiene	Sanguinity
Conviviality	Imagination	Satisfaction
Coolness	Impact	Security
Cooperation	Impartiality	Self-control

Cordiality	Independence	Selflessness
Correctness	Industry	Self-reliance
Courage	Ingenuity	Sensitivity
Courtesy	Inquisitiveness	Sensuality
Craftiness	Insightfulness	Serenity
Creativity	Inspiration	Service
Credibility	Integrity	Sexuality
Cunning	Intelligence	Sharing
Curiosity	Intensity	Shrewdness
Daring	Intimacy	Significance
Decisiveness	Intrepidness	Silence
Decorum	Introversion	Silliness
Deference	Intuition	Simplicity
Delight	Intuitiveness	Sincerity
Dependability	Intuitiveness	Skilfulness
Depth	Inventiveness	Solidarity
Desire	Investing	Solitude
Determination	Joy	Soundness

Devotion	Judiciousness	Speed
Devoutness	Justice	Spirit
Dexterity	Keenness	Spirituality
Dignity	Kindness	Spontaneity
Diligence	Knowledge	Spunk
Direction	Leadership	Stability
Directness	Learning	Stealth
Discipline	Liberation	Stillness
Discovery	Liberty	Strength
Discretion	Liveliness	Structure
Diversity	Logic	Success
Dominance	Love	Support
Dreaming	Loyalty	Supremacy
Drive	Majesty	Surprise
Duty	Making a difference	Sympathy
Dynamism	Mastery	Synergy
Eagerness	Maturity	Teamwork
Economy	Meekness	Temperance

Ecstasy	Mellowness	Thankfulness
Education	Meticulousness	Thoroughness
Effectiveness	Mindfulness	Thrift
Efficiency	Modesty	Tidiness
Elation	Motivation	Timeliness
Elegance	Mysteriousness	Traditionalism
Empathy	Neatness Nerve	Tranquillity
Encouragement	Obedience	Transcendence
Endurance	Open-mindedness	Trust
Energy	Openness	Trustworthiness
Enjoyment	Optimism	Truth
Entertainment	Order	Understanding
Enthusiasm	Organisation	Unflappability
Excellence	Originality	Uniqueness
Excitement	Outlandishness	Unity
Exhilaration	Outrageousness	Usefulness
Expectancy	Passion	Utility
Expediency	Peace	Valour

Experience	Perceptiveness	Variety
Expertise	Perfection	Victory
Exploration	Perkiness	Vigour
Expressiveness	Perseverance	Virtue
Extravagance	Persistence	Vision
Extroversion	Persuasiveness	Vitality
Exuberance	Philanthropy	Vivacity
Fairness	Piety	Warmth
Faith	Playfulness	Watchfulness
Fame	Pleasantness	
Family	Pleasure	

References

Alexander, G., & Renshaw, B. (2005). *SuperCoaching*. London: Random House Business.

Bedwell, W., Wildman, J., DiazGranados, D., Salazar, M., Kramer, W., & Salas, E. (2012). Collaboration at work: An integrative multilevel conceptualisation. *Human Resource Management Review*, *22*(2), 128-145. doi: 10.1016/j.hrmr.2011.11.007

Bluckert, P. (2008). *Psychological dimensions of executive coaching*. Maidenhead: Open University Press.

Brown, P., & Brown, V. (2012). *Neuropsychology for coaches*. Berkshire, England, McGraw-Hill Education

Chamine, S. (2016). *Positive intelligence*. Ausitn, TX: Greenleaf Book Group Press.

Dispenza, D. (2014). *You Are the Placebo*. Hay House Publishing.

Flaherty, J. (2015). *Coaching*. [Place of publication not identified]: Routledge.

Fleishman, E., Dunnette, M., Howell, W., & Alluisi, E. (1982). *Human performance and productivity*. Hillsdale, NJ: Erlbaum.

Gaffney, M. (2016). *Flourishing*. [Place of publication not identified]: Penguin Books.

Geissler, H., Hasenbein, M., Kanatouri, S., & Wegner, S. (2014). E-Coaching: Conceptual and Empirical Finding of a Virtual Coaching Programme. *International Journal Of Evidence-Based Coaching And Mentoring*, *12*(2), 165 – 187.

Goleman, D. (2006). *Emotional intelligence*. New York: Bantam Books.

Honey, P., & Mumford, A. (1986). *The manual of learning styles*. Maidenhead, Berkshire: Peter Honey.

JoVE Science Education Database. (2020). *Developmental Psychology. Habituation: Studying Infants Before They Can Talk. JoVE,* [Video]. Cambridge, MA.

Kahneman, D., & Egan, P. (2011). *Thinking, fast and slow*. New York: Random House Audio.

Kolb, D., & Fry, R. (1974). *Towards an applied theory of experiential learning*. Cambridge, Mass.: M.I.T. Alfred P. Sloan School of Management.

Levinson, D. (1986). A conception of adult development. *American Psychologist*, *41*(1), 3-13. doi: 10.1037/0003-066x.41.1.3

Maltz, M., & Powers, M. (2010). *Psycho-cybernetics*. Chatsworth, Calif.: Wilshire Book Co.

Merrick, M., Ports, K., Ford, D., Afifi, T., Gershoff, E., & Grogan-Kaylor, A. (2017). Unpacking the impact of adverse childhood experiences on adult mental health. *Child Abuse & Neglect*, *69*, 10-19. doi: 10.1016/j.chiabu.2017.03.016

Miller, K. (2015). *Global values, A new paradigm for a new world* (1st ed.). Our New Evolution LLC.

Newman, M. (2009). *Emotional capitalists*. Chichester: John Wiley & Sons.

O'Neill, M. (2013). *Executive coaching with backbone and heart*. Vancouver, B.C.: Langara College

Rogers, J. (2012). *Coaching skills*. Maidenhead: Open University Press.

Rushdie, S. (2013). *Midnight's children*. London: Vintage.

State of Remote Work 2019. (2020). Retrieved 7 April 2020, from https://buffer.com/state-of-remote-work-2019

Stein, S., & Book, H. (2011). *The EQ edge*. Mississauga, Ontario: Jossey-Bass.

Taylor, D. (2020). Trends 2018: Speed is the Heart of the Learner Experience -. https://trainingindustry.com/magazine/nov-dec-2017/trends-2018-speed-is-the-heart-of-the-learner-experience/

2018 Training Industry Report. (2020). Retrieved 10 May 2020, from https://trainingmag.com/trgmag-article/2018-training-industry-report/

Tolan, J. (2003). *Skills in person-centred counselling & psychotherapy*. London: SAGE.

Whitmore, J. (2009). *Coaching for performance*. Boston: Nicholas Brealey.

Whitworth, L., Kimsey-House, K., Kimsey-House, H., & Sandahl, P. (2010). *Co-Active Coaching*. London: Nicholas Brealey Pub.

Woollett, K., & Maguire, E. (2011). Acquiring 'the Knowledge' of London's Layout Drives Structural Brain Changes. *Current Biology*, *21*(24), 2109-2114. doi: 10.1016/j.cub.2011.11.018

Index

affirmations, 206

ARCH, 26, 101, 113, 114, 115, 121, 126, 132, 143

Auditory, 154, 155, 156

auditory digital, 154, 157, 166

belief, 9, 11, 5, 19, 45, 87, 115, 149, 167, 184, 187, 193, 194, 195, 197, 198, 199, 200, 201, 202, 203, 204, 205, 206, 207, 208

biases, 11, 27, 28, 87, 174, 186

body language, 90, 148, 150, 152, 159, 160, 161, 162, 163, 165, 180, 182

business, 12, 5, 6, 7, 9, 16, 17, 23, 39, 40, 41, 42, 43, 44, 45, 46, 49, 50, 51, 52, 53, 56, 57, 60, 61, 62, 63, 65, 68, 100, 110, 112, 164, 217, 220, 223, 225, 226, 228, 229, 247

Case Study, 58, 61, 65, 81, 105, 108, 118, 122, 127, 136, 187, 195, 216

client, 12, 2, 15, 22, 23, 30, 36, 50, 51, 52, 55, 56, 91, 92, 93, 94, 96, 109, 110, 113, 140, 144, 159, 168, 169, 170, 171, 173, 176, 177, 207, 218

coach, 9, 2, 7, 8, 14, 39, 52, 54, 56, 64, 119, 122, 123, 124, 125, 127, 128, 129, 130, 131, 136, 137, 138, 171, 172

coachee, 4, 5, 8, 10, 11, 12, 2, 3, 5, 6, 10, 11, 12, 14, 19, 22, 23, 24, 25, 26, 27, 28, 29, 30, 36, 37, 38, 46, 47, 48, 50, 51, 54, 59, 60, 61, 69, 71, 72, 81, 82, 83, 86, 87, 88, 90, 92, 93, 94, 95, 101, 102, 104, 105, 106, 107, 109, 110, 111, 112, 113, 114, 115, 116, 118, 120, 121, 122, 123, 125, 126, 127, 128, 132, 134, 135, 138, 140, 141, 142, 143, 145, 146, 147, 152, 157, 158, 159, 162, 163, 165, 166, 167, 168, 173, 174, 175, 177, 181, 182, 183, 188, 189, 191, 192, 197, 198, 199, 200, 201, 202, 203, 204, 205, 206, 208, 209, 210, 211, 212, 214, 215, 220, 221, 222, 223, 224, 235 coaching contract, 39, 111, 219, 220

collaborative coaching, 3, 8, 1, 11, 12, 13, 26, 40, 59, 69, 87, 88, 91, 111, 113, 114, 152, 163, 166, 187, 191, 195, 217, 224

competencies, 22, 32, 34, 43, 69, 112

concluding, 67, 219, 220, 222

consultancy, 1, 13, 15, 111

cost-benefit, 61, 62, 226

counselling, 9, 1, 3, 4, 13, 14, 111, 153, 249

culture, 6, 12, 39, 49, 99, 179, 196

digital, 7, 148, 157, 179, 180, 181, 222

Doer, 71, 73, 74, 82, 83, 86, 87

emotional intelligence, 5, 45, 64, 72, 128, 184

executive, 1, 5, 10, 12, 7, 9, 39, 40, 41, 42, 43, 46, 48, 50, 51, 53, 54, 55, 56, 57, 58, 60, 61, 81, 99, 105, 107, 108, 112, 120, 146, 216, 220, 228, 247, 248

feedback, 10, 11, 24, 27, 28, 52, 53, 56, 59, 75, 123, 124, 125, 128, 129, 132, 140, 141, 142, 143, 144, 145, 146, 147, 150, 222

How the mind works, 184

IGOR, 60

Intellectual, 71, 76, 77, 78, 84, 86, 87

Kinaesthetic, 155, 156, 157

leadership, 41, 44, 216, 218, 242

learn, 10, 1, 4, 39, 43, 69, 71, 72, 73, 74, 75, 76, 77, 78, 79, 80, 101, 121, 128, 148, 184, 185, 209

life coaching, 39, 43, 46, 61, 68, 70, 112

listening, 3, 20, 27, 90, 142, 148, 149, 159, 166, 167, 168, 169, 170, 172, 173, 176, 177, 178, 231 manager, 64

mentoring, 8, 1, 13, 17, 18, 20, 111

neuropsychology, 184

Observer, 71, 79, 80, 81, 82, 85, 86, 87

organisation, 8, 47, 49, 244

paraphrasing, 27, 170

perception, 57, 60, 142

plasticity, 189

positive intelligence, 184, 187

profile, 57

question, 10, 12, 24, 25, 56, 77, 91, 94, 95, 96, 98, 121, 124, 129, 157, 168, 173, 183, 195, 197, 198, 203, 210, 221

questioning, 6, 28, 36, 67, 69, 90, 91, 107, 127, 169, 189, 197, 202, 203

rapport, 37, 81, 91, 95, 111, 112, 119, 148, 150, 152, 159, 163, 164, 165, 166, 180, 183, 222

Realist, 71, 75, 76, 83, 84, 86, 87

reflecting, 27, 170, 171, 172, 210

Reflective Exercise, 13, 20, 22, 31, 33, 43, 58, 82, 86, 91, 117, 120, 140, 143, 150, 158, 159, 164, 167, 174, 175, 186, 191, 193, 196, 199, 211

reframing, 175

strategic, 9, 60, 228, 229

summarising, 27, 170, 172

therapy, 1, 13, 14, 15, 111

tone, 158

values, 50, 184, 208, 209, 210, 211, 217

visual, 155, 156

Printed in Great Britain
by Amazon